UNSTUCK
STUDY GUIDE

UNSTUCK
STUDY GUIDE

Move from Powerless to Empowered
in Your Relationships

CHARLENE BENSON

MEDIA.COM

Copyright © 2022 Charlene Benson

All rights reserved. No part of this book may be reproduced in any form or by any means—whether electronic, digital, mechanical, or otherwise—without permission in writing from the publisher, except by a reviewer, who may quote brief passages in a review.

The views and opinions expressed in this book are those of the author and do not necessarily reflect the official policy or position of Illumify Media Global.

Unless otherwise noted Scripture quotations are taken from the New King James Version®. Copyright © 1982 by Thomas Nelson. Used by permission. All rights reserved.

Scripture quotations marked ESV are taken from the ESV® Bible (The Holy Bible, English Standard Version®). Copyright © 2001 by Crossway, a publishing ministry of Good News Publishers. Used by permission. All rights reserved.

Scripture quotations marked NIV are taken from the Holy Bible, New International Version®, NIV. Copyright © 1973, 1978, 1984, 2011 by Biblica, Inc. Used by permission of Zondervan. All rights reserved worldwide. www.zondervan.com. The "NIV" and "New International Version" are trademarks registered in the United States Patent and Trademark Office by Biblica, Inc.®

Published by
Illumify Media Global
www.IllumifyMedia.com
"Let's bring your book to life!"

Library of Congress Control Number: 2022908858

Paperback ISBN: 978-1-947360-98-3

Typeset by Art Innovations (http://artinnovations.in/)
Cover design by Debbie Lewis

Printed in the United States of America

DEDICATION

This book is dedicated to my husband, Michael.
To my children, Stephen and David, and their wives, Melissa and Katie.
To my grandchildren, Joseph, Amelia, Olivia, Eliana, Ezekiel,
those in heaven, and the ones yet to be born.
To my living siblings, Conni Griffee and Curtis Dahlke,
and their spouses, Randy and Carol.
To my relatives and friends.
My hope is for all of us to be on the road together!

CONTENTS

	Acknowledgments	ix
	Introduction	xi
1.	The Others-Focused Ditch	1
2.	The Me-Focused Ditch	38
3.	What Drives Ditch Behaviors	67
4.	Switching Ditches	89
5.	Everyone Is Afraid	115
6.	Deep Ravines	126
7.	Ditching People	136
8.	Building a Path Out of the Ditch	150
9.	Stepping-Stones for Crawling Out of the Ditch	157
10.	The ABCDs of Negative Interactions	165
11.	Path to Empowerment: How to Stop Attacking and Accusing	176
12.	Path to Empowerment: How to Stop Blaming, Criticizing, Defending, and Deflecting	185
13.	From the Others-Focused Ditch to the Road	192
14.	From the Me-Focused Ditch to the Road	216
15.	On the Road	241
16.	What to Do About Fear	246
17.	Developing an Ideal Relationship	271
	Afterword: Road Trip	278
	Notes	283
	About the Author	286

ACKNOWLEDGMENTS

"If any of you lacks wisdom, let him ask God, who gives generously to all without reproach, and it will be given him." (James 1:5 ESV)

Any wisdom you may glean from *Unstuck* or this accompanying study guide comes from God's inspiration to me. Thank You, God!

I'm also deeply grateful to Rob Scuka and the late Bernard Guerney for developing Relationship Enhancement (RE) communication skills for couples. Many of the ideas in *Unstuck* spawned from what I learned from RE. Deep, sincere gratitude goes to Don and Alexandra Flecky for CoupleTalk.com, who made Relationship Enhancement skills available online to the masses.

A heartfelt thanks goes to my sister, Conni Griffee, and my friend Carolee Wise. I appreciate your candid comments, suggestions, edits, and encouragement. I couldn't have done this without you!

Thank you to Tal Smiley, who introduced me to the documentary *Before the Wrath*.

I deeply appreciate my book coach and editor, Karen Scalf Bouchard, whose expertise and hard work made this study guide user-friendly, well-written, and professional. I'm thankful to Jenna Love for copy editing, Debbie Lewis for the fabulous book cover design, and Mike Klassen and Jennifer Clark at Illumify Media Global for their help in educating me and helping me throughout the publishing process.

Finally, I'm especially thankful to my family and friends, who encouraged me during the writing process!

INTRODUCTION

The *Unstuck Study Guide* was created as a tool to help you navigate and apply the information presented in *Unstuck: Move from Powerless to Empowered in Your Relationships*. My hope is that it will speed up the process of you crawling out of the ditch that has been keeping you stuck. You've lived there long enough. Now it's time to get out and start making headway along the road!

More than ever, the internal work encouraged in my book and in this study guide is critical for the preparation of becoming the purified bride of Christ.

Let me explain.

Recently, a friend introduced me to the documentary *Before the Wrath*.[1] (You can learn more by visiting www.beforethewrath.com.) This film explains Galilean wedding customs during the time of Jesus. It also sheds important light on many things Jesus said referring to His second coming. Once I understood the customs of the time, the parable of the ten virgins as told in the Bible made much more sense to me! The Bible passage is found in Matthew 25:1–13:

> "Then the kingdom of heaven shall be likened to ten virgins who took their lamps and went out to meet the bridegroom. Now five of them were wise, and five were foolish. Those who were foolish took their lamps and took no oil with them, but the wise took oil in their vessels with their lamps. But while the bridegroom was delayed, they all slumbered and slept.
>
> "And at midnight a cry was heard: 'Behold, the bridegroom is coming; go out to meet him!' Then all those virgins arose and trimmed their lamps. And the foolish said to the wise, 'Give us some of your oil, for our lamps are going out.' But the wise answered, saying, 'No, lest there should not be enough for us and you; but go rather to those who sell, and buy for yourselves.' And while they went to buy, the bridegroom came, and those

who were ready went in with him to the wedding; and the door was shut.

"Afterward the other virgins came also, saying, 'Lord, Lord, open to us!' But he answered and said, 'Assuredly, I say to you, I do not know you.'

"Watch therefore, for you know neither the day nor the hour in which the Son of Man is coming.

The oil in verse 8 refers to the Holy Spirit. We need to be filled with the Holy Spirit in order to have enough oil in our lives to get us through the coming spiritual darkness.

Fear creates darkness in our hearts, minds, and throughout the world.

The COVID-19 virus that so heavily impacted our lives in 2020, and continues to do so, is a prime example. Without belittling the actual risks or deaths related to COVID-19, the *fear* of the virus and the resulting *isolation* had as much or more impact on many of us than the actual virus. People became so afraid to breathe that they rode bikes, drove alone in cars, or went for hikes with masks covering their noses and mouths, increasing the intake of carbon dioxide and decreasing the intake of life-sustaining oxygen.

Some have stated that this book is not for them because they don't believe fear is an issue in their lives. They don't feel an urgency to learn the twenty-four strategies for addressing fear as discussed in chapter 16. I've heard comments such as, "But I'm not a fearful person!" That may be true, *and* you still will be bombarded by stealth fears attacking you in the form of anxiety, worry, concern, irritation, uneasiness, nervousness, or dread. *All of us are affected. And the fears will do whatever they can to avoid being exposed.*

The Holy Spirit displaces fear because the Holy Spirit is love. Perfect love casts out fear (1 John 4:18). Many of our fears remain hidden from our consciousness, leaving our hearts at low capacity for the indwelling of the Spirit. That was true for me; maybe it's true at times for you too.

This workbook will help you do the deep cleaning necessary to root out those pesky fears, freeing you to open your heart fully to the love of God.

Here are some tips to getting the most from this study guide:
- The *Unstuck Study Guide* can be used in a group setting, or you can go through it on your own.
- If you are using this study guide in a group, it's important to create an environment that feels safe. To do that, have members of the group agree to confidentiality. It's also important for group members to share only their own stories with others, not the stories of other people in or outside the group. Finally, commit to not interrupting each other and not offering suggestions or solutions to others unless asked. It may be helpful to review these guidelines at the start of each meeting to keep them in the forefront of the participants' minds.
- The important work we do to become healthy and free is a lifelong process, so let go of any pressure to "complete" this guide in a short time. If you are working through these pages on your own, I encourage you to go as slow or as fast as feels comfortable. Most important, take as much time as you need on each question or section. If you are participating in a group for a set amount of time, you will benefit greatly. However, you may find that you want to return to this guide on your own and go through the exercises (or specific sections) again at your own pace. You will discover a new level of awareness and freedom each time you work through this material.
- Whether you are going through this guide in a group setting or on your own, you may decide that you need more space to write your answers than what is provided in these pages. If so, consider writing in a journal or notebook so you don't feel limited by space as you process your answers.
- You may need to take breaks from this study guide to avoid getting overloaded or burned out—or because of the emotional impact the process often has on people. No matter how long that intermission needs to be, commit to returning until you eventually complete the steps in this guide. You'll be a happier, freer person if you complete this inner work.

This guide is designed to help you find healing and freedom. As you work through the sections, you'll be empowered to recognize default behaviors in your life and in the lives of others (chapters 1 and 2), understand the fears that drive those behaviors (chapter 3), and recognize when and why you and your partner are "switching ditches" (chapter 4).

You'll more accurately discern your anger, rage, hurt, and stress (chapter 5) and how dysfunction in childhood can contribute to these painful emotions and triggers (chapter 6).

You'll discover how to assess whether to end a toxic relationship (chapter 7), then become equipped to develop a framework that will allow you to live a more balanced life by replacing automatic patterns with empowered decisions and choices (chapters 8, 9, 10, 11, and 12).

You'll gain life-changing insights into Ditch Behaviors (chapters 13 and 14), learn about the strengths that come from them (chapter 15), and discover twenty-four powerful strategies for overcoming fears (chapter 16).

Finally, you'll discover many elements that comprise an ideal relationship (chapter 17). At the end of the study guide, I'll walk you through looking in the rearview mirror and recognizing how far you've come.

My hope and prayer is that *Unstuck* and the *Unstuck Study Guide* will become reference materials you can return to time and again.

For most of our lives, we've been locked into the rules of living that were modeled and taught by our family of origin. What we learned from these rules is a mixed bag of things: some good, some not-so-good, and some downright horrid.

The good news is that we can learn new ways to interact with others, express what we want and need, and address old fears that trigger us to react in unhealthy ways.

What you will discover as you work through the *Unstuck* book and this study guide may feel overwhelming at times. It can cause many emotions to surface, including grief, as you begin to see the unhealthy patterns you've been operating from for so long, patterns that have brought suffering into your life.

This is to be expected. If you start to feel flooded, put the book down and do some journaling to help yourself understand what's going on internally. These are emotions that have been buried and need to be set free. If the emotions feel too overwhelming, consider talking with a counselor or life coach to help you process what you are experiencing.

Also, after every section you'll engage with three valuable offerings:

My prayer over you. While I may not know you by name, I have walked in your shoes and have been praying over you. The Lord knows by name every person who will at some point read these pages, and I have been asking Him even now to prepare your heart, bless you and your relationships, and empower, heal, and free you.

Conversation starters with God. As you seek Him in this process, you'll find that God is the ultimate source of your healing and freedom. Spend time with Him after every session. The conversation starters are simply suggested prompts to help make your time with Him more meaningful. The prompts are meant to enhance your connection with God, if you choose to use them.

Points to ponder in group discussion or private journaling. Talk about these with your group or process them on your own.

My prayer over you:
Dear God, I pray for every person who picks up this workbook. Fill their hearts and minds with Your love, displacing all the fears that bombard them constantly. Please help each person grow in awareness, develop an acceptance of self and others, and experience a freedom from the fears that threaten to keep us all stuck in chains. In Jesus' name, amen.

CHAPTER 1

THE OTHERS-FOCUSED DITCH

Read or reread chapter 1 in *Unstuck*.

Main Ideas

Here's a list of the main ideas you'll find in chapter 1:
- Ditch Behaviors come from flawed thinking patterns.
- A "ditch" represents an extreme in behavior.
- When we are stuck in the Others-Focused Ditch, we tend to focus on the thoughts, feelings, concerns, and desires of our partners and disregard our own thoughts, feelings, concerns, and desires.
- Each Ditch Behavior is driven by fear and feeling powerless, though we may be unaware of the fear or the feeling.
- Following are twenty-one of the most common behaviors exhibited by people who are stuck in the Others-Focused Ditch:

○ People pleaser	○ Default answer = yes
○ Readily giving up what I want	○ Difficulty making decisions
○ Walking on eggshells	○ Difficulty expressing thoughts and feelings
○ Avoiding issues	○ Tendency toward codependency
○ Blaming others	○ Acting passive
○ Feeling obligated	○ Being resentful
○ Coping through sarcasm	○ Criticizing or gossiping
○ Nursing Hurts	○ Being Passive-aggressive
○ Withdrawing	○ Shutting down
○ Feeling chaotic	○ Victim mindset
○ Self-harming	

- These behaviors are subconscious, preprogrammed, automatic, and reactionary.
- Extreme feelings of powerlessness can lead to self-harm.
- "Others-Focused Behaviors" often begin in childhood in an attempt to gain love and/or acceptance.
- Awareness is the first step of change.
- An important step toward healing: "I give myself permission to think of myself while at the same time considering the perspectives of others."

OTHERS-FOCUSED BEHAVIORS: SESSION 1

Let's start by examining where you are right now in relationships with the key people in your life. There's so much to explore in this chapter that it has been divided into five sessions.

Before we begin, I want to introduce you to a helpful technique that is often used with a type of therapy known as EMDR (Eye Movement Desensitization Reprocessing) to deal with any distressing feelings that may arise.

This technique is called a "container" and provides a safe place to store painful or distressing memories and feelings until we are ready to explore them.[1]

To do this exercise, begin by imagining a secure container—something that can be closed, yet is strong and large enough to hold every bothersome experience, word, thought, feeling, memory, image, physical sensation, sound, smell, or emotion.

In a sense, our brains do this already. Often, when we go through difficult experiences or traumas, our brain tries to help us cope by blocking out the event, minimizing ("It wasn't that bad."), denying that it ever happened, or pushing it down and slamming a figurative concrete lid on it.

What makes the container different is that we're not *denying* the pain. In fact, we're acknowledging the truth—"Painful things have happened."—while acknowledging another powerful truth at the same time: "But I can't deal with the pain all at once."

That is why we need the container: to safely store the pain until we *can or become ready to* deal with it.

As you go through this study guide and you start to experience uncomfortable sensations, distressing feelings, or anxiety, I encourage you to stop reading and imagine yourself putting those emotions into your container and closing it securely, assuring yourself that you will work on them when you are ready, whenever that may be.

By the way, your imagined container might be as simple as a shoe box or bottle with a lid. You might imagine a safe or a treasure chest. Some people envision large containers, such as a locked room, storage unit, or shipping container. I love the creative containers people come up with that work for them that also match their personalities. What's important is that it's big enough and strong enough to hold everything you need to put in it. It also needs to be secure enough that things won't leak out.

What did you choose for a container? Write it down. What color is it, and what does it look like? How big is it? What is it made of? Where is it located? What makes it secure and sealed so nothing can leak out? Because it's something you have created in your mind, you have access to this container twenty-four hours a day, seven days a week. Describe and/or draw your container in the space below:

Let's try it out! Imagine putting all your disturbing thoughts, feelings, experiences, and memories into your container. Now close it, and make sure it's sealed, then imagine walking away from the container in your mind.

Can you feel a difference? What does it feel like?

Sometimes it's a process to get everything to go in and stay in. So if it doesn't all go in at once, consider what you're afraid will happen if you put everything inside and leave it there until you are ready to deal with it. Often, naming that fear and examining the concern will help you work through the blockage. You might also consider seeking the help of a counselor or coach to assist you in identifying your thoughts, feelings, and memories.

Did it all go in? Yes ___ No___

If not, what are you afraid will happen if you put your "pain" into a container?

Keep practicing using this mental exercise until you successfully get your painful things to go inside and stay inside of the container.

Use this container any time upsetting things happen that you aren't able to deal with in the moment. You can also figuratively open it and take things out to work on as you work through this study guide. With dedication and commitment to doing this work, my hope is that you'll eventually be able to reduce the number of painful things you need to store in your container. When you're done working on a session or a question for the day, remember to put anything unresolved back into your container.

> **Is there anything you would like to put in your container? If so, do it now. Feel free to make a note of what you put away.**

Exercise: How Stuck Do You Feel Today?

Let's start by getting a sense of how stuck you are feeling right now in this moment. After all, you won't know if you've made progress by the end of the study unless you rate where you are right now.

Rate the intensity of your feelings from 1 to 10. Often, our brains will try to rationalize away intense emotions. However, the first number that pops into your head is where you're at right now. The number may seem faint or far away, but there will be a number that emerges if you allow it to.

On a scale from 1 (not very) to 10 (extremely), rate your answers based on how you feel today:

A. How stuck do you feel in life? _____
B. What is your current level of anxiety? _____
C. How fearful are you? _____

Because we often struggle to maintain harmonious relationships, there's likely at least one person with whom we have some unresolved issue. Identifying where we feel stuck, who is involved, and what we do when it happens will assist us in figuring out what to do differently.

1. Identify significant people in your life with whom you feel stuck in your relationship. Consider your mate, kids, parents, coworkers, boss, extended family, and friends. One or more people may come to mind.

2. What is the issue or conflict you wish you could change with each person?

3. Going forward, choose one person and one issue. This process may be repeated as often as you like, but you will feel less stress when you work through one relationship at a time. Ask yourself: "What keeps me from confronting that person? How has my attempt to address the issue been blocked?"

4. What situations with that person do you believe or feel you are powerless to change?

5. If you have tried to address the problem with this person, what reaction did you get when you spoke up?

6. If you have not tried to address the problem, why not? What are you afraid will happen if you do?

**Is there anything you would like to put in your container? If so, do it now.
Feel free to make a note of what you put away.**

In our session today, we looked at the state of things right now. You put words to what's been going on, and maybe it's been that way for a long time. This was a big step! Way to go!

This is significant because we can't deal effectively with a problem until we have named it.

Now, take a deep breath!

It's possible that identifying in writing your emotions and challenges has made your situation feel even more hopeless. Don't despair!

I assure you that very soon we're going to discover solutions that will bring you healing and relief. And doesn't it feel just a tiny bit freeing to be able to vocalize your situation, to know that the goal is to discover a new pathway, and that you've just completed the first step on that journey?

Remember, you may go as slow or as fast as you'd like. You can stay in the shallow end or dive in deep. It's your journey. Many of us need to take it slow because we're just getting started in this process of healing; whereas others have already come a long way in their recovery from life's hurts and are ready to delve in.

The wonderful thing about God is that He doesn't force us to go any faster than we are ready to go. Satan, on the other hand, has forced us into all kinds of things against our will. Maybe it will help to repeat the following prayer every day until we make it to Session 2:

> *Dear God, I feel so powerless in my situation that it feels hopeless to even pray about it. This problem seems so overwhelming that anything I do, including praying, won't seem to even scratch the surface or make any difference. Help me in my powerlessness! In 2 Corinthians 12:10, You say that when I am weak, I am strong in You. Well, I feel as helpless as a baby, and I desperately need Your strength right now! Please, show up in ways I don't even know how to ask. In Jesus' name, amen.*

My prayer over you:

Dear God, I pray for this dear reader as they embark on this healing journey. Make Your presence felt to them this very moment. Fill their heart with peace and joy as they begin to anticipate the good things You have in store for them. In Jesus' name, amen.

Conversation starters with God:

Now it's your turn to pray. Find a quiet place. Bring a journal and pen if you enjoy writing your prayers. Above all, be prepared to listen to what God has to say to you in response. And because prayer is a conversation with someone who knows and loves you, here are a few conversations starters to get the ball rolling:

Dear God,
- What would You have me take away from today's session?
- I'd love to see people in my life the way You see them. Show me how You see them.
- Have I been in a ditch? I'd love to hear Your thoughts on that.

Points to ponder in group discussion or private journaling:

1. As you interacted with God, what did you hear from Him?

2. What was the biggest aha moment from this section?

3. Based on what you learned about the Others-Focused Ditch, identify one action you can take that would be helpful (reminder: "noticing" counts as an action).

OTHERS-FOCUSED BEHAVIORS: SESSION 2

Today we're going to look at seven Others-Focused Ditch Behaviors. Because awareness is the first step of change, our goal for the next three sessions is to gain understanding of our default behaviors.

By the way, we're not yet at the point of changing anything—that will come soon. Right now, I simply want you to notice what is causing you to spin your wheels and to wonder why you're not getting anywhere.

Please lay aside any self-criticism as you do this. Pretend you're in a theater watching a movie, and you're curious about what the main characters are doing—the individuals you are observing on the imaginary screen are you and the people in your life.

We'll talk about the next step in future chapters. For now, observe and take note of when and how the following show up in your life. Note whether you find yourself defaulting in that way or if someone else in your life is doing that, then name that person(s). We'll review your responses in a later chapter.

1. People-Pleasing
- Check this box if you see this behavior in yourself: ☐
- Check this box if you see this behavior in other people in your life: ☐
- If you see this behavior in others in your life, name them:

Give an example:

- If you see this behavior in yourself, what feelings accompany this behavior?

- Does your focus on pleasing others feel good, or do you sometimes feel resentful or trapped?

2. The Default Answer is *Yes*.
- Check this box if you see this behavior in yourself: ☐
- Check this box if you see this behavior in other people in your life: ☐
- If you see this behavior in others in your life, name them:

- On what topics do you tend to automatically respond with a yes to others?

3. Readily Giving Up What I Want
- Check this box if you see this behavior in yourself: ☐
- Check this box if you see this behavior in other people in your life: ☐
- If you see this behavior in others in your life, name them:

- Provide a recent example:

    If you see this behavior in yourself, describe a time when you advocated for what you wanted. What was the result?

4. Difficulty Making Decisions
- Check this box if you see this behavior in yourself: ☐
- Check this box if you see this behavior in other people in your life: ☐
- If you see this behavior in others in your life, name them:

- On which topics is decision-making difficult?

- What typically happens in those situations?

5. Walking on Eggshells
- Check this box if you see this behavior in yourself: ☐
- Check this box if you see it in other people in your life: ☐
- If you see this behavior in others in your life, name them:

- When you're walking on eggshells, is it related to specific subjects? Name these subjects.

- Do you feel like you walk on eggshells around certain people frequently? Who?

- Describe a time when you addressed a difficult subject in spite of your fears about how the other person would react. What happened?

6. Difficulty Expressing Thoughts and Feelings
- Check this box if you see this behavior in yourself: ☐
- Check this box if you see this behavior in other people in your life: ☐

- If you see this behavior in others in your life, name them:

- Who in your life seems to have difficulty expressing feelings or opinions?

- On which topics does this tend to occur?

7. Avoiding Conflict
- Check this box if you see this behavior in yourself: ☐
- Check this box if you see this behavior in other people in your life: ☐
- If you see this behavior in others in your life, name them:

- What topics seem most difficult to discuss?

- Name an experience when a topic that would typically be avoided was addressed. What was the outcome?

> **Is there anything you would like to put in your container? If so, do it now. Feel free to make a note of what you put away.**

Look back at your responses.
How many of those did you mark as true for you? _____
How many behaviors did you indicate observing in someone else? _____

 I'm so proud of you for getting this far! Your journey into greater awareness continues. If you're like me, you've been heavily invested in avoiding how powerless you felt and how afraid you were that there seemed to be no other course of action. If you are like my spouse, key people in your life have driven you crazy because they behaved this way around you. That is what kept the two of us locked into repeating ditchy behaviors. But it was the only way we knew how to react!

 At first, just noticing what I did for so long brought up feelings of resentment because others didn't take me into consideration in the same way I looked out for and considered them. On the other hand, some of you feel frustrated and angry when people in your life tend to behave in this caretaking manner.

My prayer over you:

Dear God, I pray for this dear reader as they begin to identify patterns that have held them back. It's possible they have felt powerless in the past to change relationship dynamics that have caused suffering. I ask that You press on their hearts that even when we feel powerless to change, we can do all things when we invite You into our lives and rely on Your strength to move through us. In Jesus' name, amen.

Conversation starters with God:

Now it's your turn to pray. Find a quiet place. Bring a journal and pen if you enjoy writing your prayers. Above all, be prepared to listen to what God has to say to you in response. And because prayer is a conversation with someone who knows and loves you, I've provided a few conversations starters to get the ball rolling:

Dear God,
- Sometimes I feel like I've been stuck forever. Please renew a sense of hope in my heart. Where can I find that hope?
- Sometimes I'm not even sure how I feel. But You know me even better than I know myself. What do I need to discover about myself? Teach me to value my feelings.
- Sometimes it's hard to fathom what You can do to transform any of this. What do I need to hear from You to help me trust You more?

Points to ponder in group discussion or private journaling:
1. As you interacted with God, what did you hear from Him?

2. What was the biggest aha moment from this section?

3. Based on what you learned in this session, identify one action you can take that would be helpful (reminder: "noticing" counts as an action).

OTHERS-FOCUSED BEHAVIORS: SESSION 3

Today, we will look at the middle seven Others-Focused Ditch Behaviors: numbers 8–14. We continue our journey of exploring our default behaviors and discovering when they crop up in our lives and with whom.

Remember that our task at this point remains the same: to notice what is going on with others around us and within ourselves. We don't want to go too fast and get overwhelmed. If we do that, we'll give up and quit, then we'll stay stuck. Our goal at this point is to gain awareness of what has been going on (something most of our parents had no opportunity to do).

Let's return to the theater where we observed our own life as if watching a movie. Before we go inside, remember to remove and check your cloak of self-judgment! Simply notice with whom you find you are observing or experiencing these behaviors:

8. Codependence (trying to save or "fix" others in order to feel needed; putting others' needs before your own)
- Check this box if you see this behavior in yourself: ☐
- Check this box if you see this behavior in other people in your life: ☐
- If you see this behavior in others in your life, name them:

- What characteristics make it seem codependent?

9. Blaming
- Check this box if you see this behavior in yourself: ☐
- Check this box if you see this behavior in other people in your life: ☐
- If you see this behavior in others in your life, name them:

- Who do you blame for your situation?

- What exactly do you blame them for? Or, in what ways do you feel blamed?

- Who blames you for something?

- What did you do to cause the problem?

- What did they do to cause the problem?

10. Being Passive
- Check this box if you see this behavior in yourself: ☐
- Check this box if you see this behavior in other people in your life: ☐
- If you see this behavior in others in your life, name them:

- Provide examples of what being passive looks like for you:

11. Feeling Obligated
- Check this box if you see this behavior in yourself: ☐
- Check this box if you see this behavior in other people in your life: ☐
- If you see this behavior in others in your life, name them:

- What do others say or do that makes you feel obligated to do what they say?

- In what ways might you imply that others are obligated to do what you say?

- With whom does the feeling carry the most intensity?

12. Being Resentful
- Check this box if you see this behavior in yourself: ☐
- Check this box if you see this behavior in other people in your life: ☐
- If you see this behavior in others in your life, name them:

- What significant experiences have left you feeling resentful?

- Toward whom do you feel the most resentment?

13. Being Sarcastic
- Check this box if you see this behavior in yourself: ☐
- Check this box if you see this behavior in other people in your life: ☐
- Who in your life tends to make sarcastic remarks?

- Around what topics does the sarcasm tend to revolve?

14. Being Critical and/or Gossipy
- Check this box if you see this behavior in yourself: ☐
- Check this box if you see this behavior in other people in your life: ☐
- If you see this behavior in others in your life, name them:

- What critical remarks have you recently thought or said about others?

- What critical remarks have you heard others say about you?

- Who tends to be the most critical of you?

> **Is there anything you would like to put in your container? If so, do it now.
> Feel free to make a note of what you put away.**

Now it's time to look back and tally up your responses.
How many of those did you mark as true for you? _____
How many times did you indicate observing this behavior in someone else? _____

That was a lot to think about, and you did it! I'm glad you're on this journey. Examining our behaviors is how we make the world a better place. We start within our own circle, figure out what we can do differently, then implement the changes.

It's like dropping a pebble in a pond. The first plunk is small, but the ripples steadily expand outward and eventually encompass the entire body of water. This is the effect change will have in your life and in the lives of all whom you touch.

My prayer over you:

Dear God, I pray for this dear reader as they grow in awareness of their own behaviors, as well as the behaviors of others. Please allow these exercises to create a sense of hope and empowerment instead of judgement or despair. Encourage my friend, dear Jesus. In Your name I pray, amen.

Conversation starters with God:

Now it's your turn to pray. Find a quiet place. Bring a journal and pen if you enjoy writing your prayers. Above all, be prepared to listen to what God has to say to you in response. And because prayer is a conversation with someone who knows and loves you, here are a few conversations starters to get the ball rolling:

Dear God,
- As I see patterns in my own behavior that have been less than helpful, it's tempting to be hard on myself. But I don't want to do that. I want to begin to see myself as You see me. What would You like to tell me so that I may see myself in a more positive light?
- I understand that conviction is from the Holy Spirit, but guilt and shame are from the Accuser. Remind me of times when You convicted me and when the Accuser guilted and shamed me. What examples will show me the difference?
- Sometimes I've blamed myself for the bad things that have happened to me and ended up feeling negative about myself. But the opinion about *me* that really matters is Your opinion. What would you like to tell me?

Points to ponder in group discussion or private journaling:

1. As you interacted with God, what did you hear from Him?

2. What was the biggest aha moment from this section?

3. Based on what you learned in this session, identify one action you can take that would be helpful (reminder: "noticing" counts as an action).

OTHERS–FOCUSED BEHAVIORS: SESSION 4

You're already a lot more aware than you were before you started this journey! Are you noticing how common these reactions are? It's almost like we were once zombies, moving mindlessly through life until we woke up and found ourselves at the bottom of a ditch!

In this section, we're going to look at the last seven Others-Focused Ditch Behaviors: numbers 15–21. We'll continue our journey of exploring the default behaviors at play in our lives, discovering when they crop up and with whom.

Remember that our task at this point is simply to notice what's happening around us. We have the rest of our lives to work on changing these behaviors. The following reactions reveal a more intense feeling of powerlessness as we explore what lies deeper in the ditch.

Let's return to our imaginary theater where we observe the movie of our own life on the silver screen and notice the "scripted" behaviors people play out. Remember to take off your cloak of self-judgment and check it before you enter! We're still in observation mode. Just take note of when you find others or yourself reacting in the following ways.

15. Nursing Hurts
- Check this box if you see this behavior in yourself: ☐
- Check this box if you see this behavior in other people in your life: ☐
- If you see this behavior in others in your life, name them:

- What makes you feel hurt?

- Who has hurt you?

16. Being Passive-Aggressive
- Check this box if you see this behavior in yourself: ☐
- Check this box if you see this behavior in other people in your life: ☐
- Name some people in your life who tend to be passive-aggressive?

- What do their behaviors look like?

17. Withdrawing
- Check this box if you see this behavior in yourself: ☐
- Check this box if you see this behavior in other people in your life: ☐
- Who tends to withdraw?

- What topics are involved when that happens?

18. Shutting down
- Check this box if you see this behavior in yourself: ☐
- Check this box if you see this behavior in other people in your life: ☐
- If you see this behavior in others in your life, name them:

- Recall a time when either you or someone else shut down during conflict:

- What brought on the reaction?

19. Experiencing Chaos
- Check this box if you see this behavior in yourself: ☐

- Check this box if you see this behavior in other people in your life: ☐

- If you see this behavior in others in your life, name them:

- What part or parts of your life or the life of others feels disorganized or chaotic to you?

- What chaotic behaviors do you wish could be eliminated?

20. Playing the Victim
- Check this box if you see this behavior in yourself: ☐
- Check this box if you see this behavior in other people in your life: ☐
- Who in your life acts like a victim?
- What does their victimhood look like?

21. Wanting to Self-Harm

- Check this box if you see this behavior in yourself: ☐
- Check this box if you see this behavior in other people in your life: ☐
- If you see this behavior in others in your life, name them:

- What circumstances led *you* to have self-harming thoughts, suicidal ideations, or to engage in some form of self-harm?

- What circumstances led *others* close to you to have self-harming thoughts, suicidal ideations, or to engage in some form of self-harm?

- What did you think or do in response to your behaviors and/or the behaviors of another?

> **Is there anything you would like to put in your container? If so, do it now. Feel free to make a note of what you put away.**

Once again, look back at your responses.
How many of those did you mark as true for you? _____
How many times did you identify this behavior in someone else? _____

You've made progress already on this journey to become unstuck. Congratulations!

My prayer over you:
Dear God, I pray for this dear reader as they gain a better understanding into how they respond when they feel powerless and afraid but often don't recognize it. Please help them to begin to see these patterns without judgement of themselves or others. Instead, fill them with a growing sense of anticipation to see what healing and good things You have in store for them. In Jesus' name, amen.

Conversation starters with God:
Now it's your turn to pray. Find a quiet place. Bring a journal and pen if you enjoy writing your prayers. Above all, be prepared to listen to what God has to say

to you in response. And because prayer is a conversation with someone who knows and loves you, here are a few conversations starters to get the ball rolling:

Dear God,
- I haven't always realized how powerless and afraid I have felt. You tell me in Your Word that You don't want me to be afraid. That's easier said than done. What is the first step I can take to begin to rid myself of my fears?
- Have I been passive-aggressive toward those I love? If so, show me. What kinds of behaviors or comments have been passive-aggressive? What is one thing You want me to change?
- What do You most want me to take away from today's session?

Points to ponder in group discussion or private journaling:
1. As you interacted with God, what did you hear from Him?

2. What was the biggest aha moment from this section?

3. Based on what you learned in this session, identify one action you can take that would be helpful (reminder: "noticing" counts as an action).

OTHERS-FOCUSED BEHAVIORS: SESSION 5

Today we wrap up chapter 1 by reflecting on the bigger picture. We'll end by pinpointing the first behavior we'd like to eliminate from our lives. Notice with the Others-Focused (OF) behaviors, the approach tends to be indirect, oblique, and passive. In this ditch, people go to great lengths to avoid hurting or upsetting others.

Eastern cultures hold honoring others in high esteem and strive to save face at all costs. Though other cultures may approach things differently, people in Western cultures who are Others-Focused also try very hard to avoid saying or doing things they believe might be hurtful to others.

That's why OFs go out of their way to couch any negative comments in lots of fluff or leaves (because they're beating around the bush). Direct confrontation, to them, seems disrespectful and hurtful. They don't want anyone's feelings to be hurt and would rather bear the hurt silently than argue.

Therefore, destructive behavior becomes self-directed. During childhood, OFs were often conditioned to give up their power and relinquish what they wanted, and their Ditch Behaviors reflect that feeling of powerlessness. I had no idea my behaviors contributed to me feeling stuck! I thought it was the fault of others!

Looking back through the previous sessions, add up the number of times you identified these behaviors in yourself, then calculate the total number of times you identified these behaviors in others:

Behaviors	You	Others
1–7		
8–14		
15–21		
Total:		

Now, add up the total for all twenty-one Others-Focused Ditch Behaviors. If you marked more as being true for you, this is your Ditch of Choice (not that it was a conscious choice). It simply means it's the ditch you tend to default to more often.

1. Who in your life engages in OF behaviors more often, you or others?

2. Which OF (Others-Focused) Ditch Behavior do you find most irritating and would like to see eliminated first?

3. What thoughts, feelings, concerns, and desires do you have that you have been ignoring?

4. What aha moments, deeper realizations, or big take-aways did you gain from working through this chapter?

5. What other behaviors do you think could be added to the Others-Focused list?

> **Is there anything you would like to put in your container? If so, do it now.
> Feel free to make a note of what you put away.**

The fact that you're here now means that you have already begun a new journey! Your eyes have been opened to behaviors that were previously hidden from your conscious awareness. You're already not as powerless as you used to be, even though we're only at the first stage of becoming aware and haven't yet learned any strategies for crawling out of the ditch.

For the first few chapters, the "new behavior" is noticing when you or someone else engages in a Ditch Behavior. Instead of keeping track of the times you forgot to notice, keep tally of the times you remembered. An easy way to record your progress can be done in the calendar or Notes app on your phone. Mark every time you remember. You'll feel much better about your progress as a result.

At the end of the week, tally up how many times you remembered to notice these behaviors in yourself or in others:

Sunday __ Monday__ Tuesday __ Wednesday __ Thursday__ Friday__ Saturday__
___ = **Total**

Celebrate your progress at the end of each chapter, even if it's in a small way. Aim to gradually increase your weekly totals of increased awareness.

Practice recognizing the all-too-familiar feeling of fear and powerlessness in the moment (which usually masks as anxiety, depression, hurt, stress, or anger), then remind yourself that we have a God who is all-powerful even in our most powerless moments. When we only see walls and rocks with no escape route, that's precisely the time to confess those feelings to God, calling on Him to make a way where there seems to be no way.

My prayer over you:

Dear God, I pray for this dear reader as they begin to see deep seated, preprogrammed, automatic behaviors that have there for years. Thank You for raising their awareness and for bringing the root of these behaviors—which is fear—into the light. In Jesus' name, amen.

Conversation starters with God:

Now it's your turn to pray. Find a quiet place. Bring a journal and pen if you enjoy writing your prayers. Above all, be prepared to listen to what God has to say to you in response. And because prayer is a conversation with someone who knows and loves you, here are a few conversations starters to get the ball rolling:

Dear God,
- What do You most want for me to take away from today's session?
- I haven't always valued myself, my boundaries, my thoughts, my convictions well. Reveal to me an image or phrase that will help me to see myself as You see me.
- Reveal to me any resentments I'm harboring toward others. What would You like for me to do with these feelings right now?
- Please show me when and how have I reacted out of fear and powerlessness?

Points to ponder in group discussion or private journaling:
1. As you interacted with God, what did you hear from Him?

2. What was the biggest aha moment from this section?

3. Based on what you learned in this session, identify one action you can take that would be helpful (reminder: "noticing" counts as an action).

CHAPTER 2

THE ME-FOCUSED DITCH

Read or reread chapter 2 in *Unstuck*.

Main Ideas

Here is a list of the main ideas you'll find in chapter 2:
- Others-Focused people tend to think their problems are the result of Me-Focused people.
- Others-Focused people tend not to see their own issues.
- In the Me-Focused Ditch, we focus on our own thoughts, feelings, concerns, and desires and disregard those of others.
- There are twenty-one common behaviors that are subconscious, preprogrammed, automatic reactions.

  - Being selfish
  - Being a perfectionist
  - Difficulty seeing others' perspectives
  - Manipulating
  - Controlling
  - Having high expectations
  - Being angry
  - Threatening behaviors
  - Attacking and accusing
  - Being addicted
  - Harming others
  - Default answer = no
  - Needing to be right
  - Demanding behavior
  - Criticizing
  - Being vocal about feelings and wants
  - Feeling disappointed
  - Demeaning words and behaviors
  - Yelling
  - Being rigid
  - Physical attacks

- People in the Me-Focused (MF) Ditch cannot see others.
- Each behavior is driven by hidden fear and feeling powerless.
- Extreme MF powerlessness can lead to harming others.
- MF behaviors developed in childhood, often during chaotic or traumatic moments, leaving that person feeling abandoned or powerless to do anything about their situation.
- Healing starts when we begin focusing on our own predicament instead of focusing on the behavior of others.

ME-FOCUSED BEHAVIORS: SESSION 1

We now turn our attention in this chapter to behaviors characteristic of the Me-Focused Ditch. In this first of five sessions, we'll begin with an overview.

Me-Focused Ditch Behaviors are also extremes to which we default when we don't know what else to do in a situation. Often, we're balanced and on the road. However, since this book is about becoming unstuck, we want to identify when we *are* stuck, which is the first step in finding the solution to the problem.

Sometimes, we think we're doing fine and don't even know we're stuck. Or maybe you are not stuck at this point in your life. If that's the case, this study will still be beneficial as you discover how to respond more effectively to people in your life who are stuck. Identifying what happens and who is involved will assist you in figuring out what you can do differently.

When you're done working on a session or a question for the day, remember to put anything unresolved into the container that we discussed at the beginning of chapter 1.

For each of the following behaviors, note the circumstances, what the behavior looks like, and who tends to exhibit the action described. Was it your mate, parents, children, or you?

1. Who in your life do you consider to be Me-Focused?

2. What characteristics do they exhibit that makes you think that?

3. In which circumstances does Me-Focused Behavior seem to be most evident, either in you or in someone you know?

4. What do you wish would be different in others? In yourself?

It's just as important to see what's going on in this ditch as it is in the Others-Focused Ditch. That way we gain a well-rounded understanding of how behaviors emanating from both ditches affect our reactions.

We want to identify areas in which extreme behaviors show up, whether in the lives of others or in ourselves. If the questions seem challenging, it's because they are! However, freedom doesn't come without a struggle.

As I mentioned in the introduction, please put judgment of others and self aside. Awareness of the dynamics that have been going on around us for centuries is dawning. Like an actual sunrise, it takes time for the darkness to give way to the ever-lightening shades of gray before the bright light of the sun breaks forth on the horizon.

We have been triggered by one another, which has kept us locked into repeating ditchy behaviors. Doing so was the only way we knew how to react!

I'm grateful you stayed with this study to gain a more in-depth understanding of Me-Focused Ditch Behaviors. I think you'll be glad you did too! Not many people are willing to take a hard look at their own relationship dynamics.

At this point, you may be experiencing some anger, hurt, or other feelings at the realization of what has been operating under the surface for so long in your life. That's understandable! You'll learn how to resolve those feelings later on in this book, so keep plugging away!

> **Is there anything you would like to put in your container? If so, do it now. Feel free to make a note of what you put away.**

My prayer over you:

Dear God, I pray for this dear reader as they may be experiencing feelings of frustration, anger, or disappointment. I ask that You give them a sense of hope and peace, and remove any doubts they may be entertaining that whisper lies, saying change will never happen. Remind them of Your transforming powers and that Your desire for them is freedom from these hurts. In Jesus' name, amen.

Conversation starters with God:

Now it's your turn to pray. Find a quiet place. Bring a journal and pen if you enjoy writing your prayers. Above all, be prepared to listen to what God has to say to you in response. And because prayer is a conversation with someone who knows and loves you, here are a few conversations starters to get the ball rolling:

Dear God,
- How have I been trying to change or control the behaviors of people around me? Reveal to me ways I've been trying to protect myself by manipulating people or circumstances.
- What do You most want me to take away from today's session?
- In what areas of my life do I need more effective strategies? What do You have in mind for me?

Points to ponder in group discussion or private journaling:

1. As you interacted with God, what did you hear from Him?

2. What was the biggest aha moment from this section?

3. Based on what you learned in this session, identify one action you can take that would be helpful (reminder: "noticing" counts as an action).

ME-FOCUSED BEHAVIORS: SESSION 2

In this session, we will take a closer look at the first seven Me-Focused Ditch Behaviors. For each of the following, note how key people in your life (such as children, parents, neighbors, friends, coworkers, television characters, and particularly those who live with you) engage in the following actions. Give an example of what each behavior looks like, and note who tends to gravitate toward this ditch.

Remember to lay aside any judgment or self-criticism by pretending you're in a theater, watching curiously about what the main characters are doing, except the individuals you are observing on the imaginary screen are the people in your life.

When you're done working on a session or a question for the day, remember to put anything unresolved back into your container.

1. **Being Selfish**
    - Check this box if you see this behavior in yourself: ☐
    - Check this box if you see this behavior in other people in your life: ☐
    - If you see this behavior in others in your life, name them:

    - What does selfishness look like in your family?

2. **The Automatic Default Answer is *No***
    - Check this box if you see this behavior in yourself: ☐
    - Check this box if you see this behavior in other people in your life: ☐

- If you see this behavior in others in your life, name them:

- On what topics does the automatic no response tend to show up?

3. Being a Perfectionist
- Check this box if you see this behavior in yourself: ☐
- Check this box if you see this behavior in other people in your life: ☐
- If you see this behavior in others in your life, name them:

- What in your life do you feel must be perfect?

4. Needing to Be Right
- Check this box if you see this behavior in yourself: ☐
- Check this box if you see this behavior in other people in your life: ☐

- If you see this behavior in others in your life, name them:

- Who in your life has a hard time admitting when he/she is wrong?

- On what topics does this seem to be most problematic?

5. **Difficulty Seeing the Perspectives of Others**
   - Check this box if you see this behavior in yourself: ☐
   - Check this box if you see this behavior in other people in your life: ☐
   If you see this behavior in others in your life, name them:

- On what topics do they or you need to be right?

6. **Being Demanding**
   Check this box if you see this behavior in yourself: ☐
   Check this box if you see this behavior in other people in your life: ☐
   If you see this behavior in others in your life, name them:

- Where do these behaviors show up most often?

7. **Being Manipulative**
   Check this box if you see this behavior in yourself: ☐
   Check this box if you see this behavior in other people in your life: ☐
   If you see this behavior in others in your life, name them:

- What does manipulation look like in your life?

Look back at your responses.
How many of those did you mark as true for you? _____
How many times did you identify these behaviors in someone else? _____

At first, noticing these ways of reacting can bring up painful feelings. You may even experience such discomfort that you want to turn to your favorite coping mechanism to escape those feelings. Work, substance abuse, relationships, food, sleep, exercise, or video games are all popular ways we avoid how we feel, keeping ourselves stuck. These behaviors help protect us from the emotional pain we experienced as a child when we felt abandoned, belittled, ashamed, or unaccepted and didn't know a better way of coping.[1]

> **Is there anything you would like to put in your container? If so, do it now. Feel free to make a note of what you put away.**

By understanding what it looks like to be in the ditch, you are discovering the pathway out. I'm glad you stayed with me this far, and I guarantee you will eventually be glad you went through the effort. You have begun an unrelenting, positive ripple effect on every life you touch!

My prayer over you:
Dear God, I pray for the dear reader going through this process. It's completely normal to feel overwhelmed or sad. If these emotions arise, I ask You to surround my friend with Your love and comfort. Help my friend to trust You and rest in You through this healing journey. In Jesus' name, amen.

THE ME-FOCUSED DITCH

Conversation starters with God:

Now it's your turn to pray. Find a quiet place. Bring a journal and pen if you enjoy writing your prayers. Above all, be prepared to listen to what God has to say to you in response. And because prayer is a conversation with someone who knows and loves you, here are a few conversations starters to get the ball rolling:

Dear God,
- Relying on my warped strategies to protect myself has left me feeling frustrated and unsatisfied. You have something so much better for me. Reveal to me what it is.
- What do You most want me to take away from today's session?
- Are there hurts I need to grieve? Reveal to me what I need to grieve at this time with You by my side.

Points to ponder in group discussion or private journaling:

1. As you interacted with God, what did you hear from Him?

2. What was the biggest aha moment from this section?

3. Based on what you learned in this session, identify one action you can take that would be helpful (reminder: "noticing" counts as an action).

ME-FOCUSED BEHAVIORS: SESSION 3

In our third session, we'll continue the discovery of how ditchy behaviors play out in your life. When engaging in Me-Focused Behaviors, we consider only our own thoughts, feelings, concerns, and desires. And like Others-Focused Behaviors, Me-Focused Behaviors are often rooted in childhood.

These ditchy behaviors aren't new. They've been around since you began learning coping mechanisms and relational survival skills. The truth is, these behaviors impact everything. We either behave in these negative ways or get into a relationship with someone who acts accordingly.

When you're done working on a session or a question for the day, put anything unresolved back into your container. Remember to lay aside any self-criticism as you do this by imagining you're in a theater, watching and curious about what the main characters are doing, only the individuals you are observing on the imaginary screen are the people in your life.

8. **Being Critical**
    Check this box if you see this behavior in yourself: ☐
    Check this box if you see this behavior in other people in your life: ☐
- If you see this behavior in others in your life, name them:

- When you think of criticism, what negative remarks come to mind?

THE ME-FOCUSED DITCH

- Whose voice(s) do you most often hear?

9. **Being Controlling**
   Check this box if you see this behavior in yourself: ☐
   Check this box if you see this behavior in other people in your life: ☐
   If you see this behavior in others in your life, name them:

   In what ways does being controlling show up in your life?

   What situations or people seem out of control in your life?

10. **Being Vocal About Feelings and Wants**
    Check this box if you see this behavior in yourself: ☐
    Check this box if you see this behavior in other people in your life: ☐

- If you see this behavior in others in your life, name them:

- On what topics does this most often seem to be the case?

11. Having High Expectations
- Check this box if you see this behavior in yourself: ☐
- Check this box if you see this behavior in other people in your life: ☐
- If you see this behavior in others in your life, name them:

- What areas of your life are held to high expectations?

12. Feeling Disappointment
Check this box if you see this behavior in yourself: ☐
Check this box if you see this behavior in other people in your life: ☐

- If you see this behavior in others in your life, name them:

- In what areas of your life does disappointment seem to show up most frequently? (school, work, etc.)

13. Becoming Angry
- Check this box if you see this behavior in yourself: ☐
- Check this box if you see this behavior in other people in your life: ☐
- If you see this behavior in others in your life, name them:

- What circumstances seem to bring about angry reactions?

14. Being Demeaning
- Check this box if you see this behavior in yourself: ☐
- Check this box if you see this behavior in other people in your life: ☐
- If you see this behavior in others in your life, name them:

- Describe a demeaning experience you endured:

> **Is there anything you would like to put in your container? If so, do it now. Feel free to make a note of what you put away.**

Once again, look back at your responses.

How many of those did you mark as true for you? ____

How times did you indicate that you observed these behaviors in someone else? ____

My prayer over you:

Dear God, I pray for this dear reader as they grapple with behaviors that have been unhelpful at best and destructive at worst. Please lead them toward responses that are rooted in Your love rather than fear. Your love is perfect, and it casts out every fear when we recognize it and give it to You. In Jesus' name, amen.

Conversation starters with God:

Now it's your turn to pray. Find a quiet place. Bring a journal and pen if you enjoy writing your prayers. Above all, be prepared to listen to what God has to say to you in response. And because prayer is a conversation with someone who knows and loves you, here are a few conversations starters to get the ball rolling:

Dear God,
- I don't like these behaviors—in myself or others. As I consider the damage that has already been done, I feel numerous difficult emotions. Help me sort out what I feel. What can I do about it?
- What do You most want me to take away from today's session?
- This seems too big for even you, even though I know it's not. Show me one thing You can help me change.

Points to ponder in group discussion or private journaling:

1. As you interacted with God, what did you hear from Him?

2. What was the biggest aha moment from this section?

3. Based on what you learned in this session, identify one action you can take that would be helpful (reminder: "noticing" counts as an action).

ME-FOCUSED BEHAVIORS: SESSION 4

Today, we will look at the last seven Me-Focused Ditch Behaviors. These are more extreme reactions driven from deep feelings of powerlessness and hidden fears, which often lurk outside our awareness. Most people have experienced these at some point in their lives. If you grew up in a house where emotional chaos occurred frequently, it is likely you adopted some of these reactions to attempt to regain control when life felt out of control.

More than ever, during this session, please put aside judgement and self-condemnation. We need all the courage we can muster to look at these dynamics that happen all too often so we can experience better lives—spiritually, emotionally, and relationally. This exercise is about noticing and becoming aware. You may need help and support as you go through this. If you do, please reach out to a trusted friend, recovery group, counselor, or life coach.

When you're done working on a session or a question for the day, put anything unresolved back into your container.

15. Threatening
- Check this box if you see this behavior in yourself: ☐
- Check this box if you see this behavior in other people in your life: ☐

If you see this behavior in others in your life, name them:

- Describe a time when a threat was levied:

- How often do threats from others tend to occur?

- What types of consequences were threatened for noncompliance?

16. Yelling
- Check this box if you see this behavior in yourself: ☐
- Check this box if you see this behavior in other people in your life: ☐
- If you see this behavior in others in your life, name them:

- What topics trigger you to yell?

- What topics trigger others to yell at you?

17. Attacking & Accusing
- Check this box if you see this behavior in yourself: ☐
- Check this box if you see this behavior in other people in your life: ☐
- If you see this behavior in others in your life, name them:

- What do people say or do to you that feels like an attack or accusation?

18. Becoming Rigid
- Check this box if you see this behavior in yourself: ☐
- Check this box if you see this behavior in other people in your life: ☐
- If you see this behavior in others in your life, name them:

- On what topics do the rules in your life seem unbending and/or extreme?

- Who levies them? (It can be an individual, a group, or an organization.)

19. Becoming Addicted
- Check this box if you see this behavior in yourself: ☐
- Check this box if you see this behavior in other people in your life: ☐
- If you see this behavior in others in your life, name them:

- What types of addictions exist in your family?

20. Physical Attacks
- Check this box if you see this behavior in yourself: ☐
- Check this box if you see this behavior in other people in your life: ☐
- If you see this behavior in others in your life, name them:

- Note a time when a physical attack took place:

   What brought it on?

   Approximately how often do physical attacks like this occur?

- Who tends to be the attacker?

21. Harming Others
- Check this box if you see this behavior in yourself: ☐
- Check this box if you see this behavior in other people in your life: ☐
- If you see this behavior in others in your life, name them:

- How often does harm to others tend to occur?

- Who caused harm in the past?

- Who currently causes harm?

Note: After this segment in particular, it's especially important to put feelings and emotions that have come up into your container.

> **Is there anything you would like to put in your container? If so, do it now. Feel free to make a note of what you put away.**

Once again, look back at your responses.

How many of those did you mark as true for you? ____

How many times did you indicate observing the behavior in someone else? ____

Now let's find out the total you marked "You" and how many of the Me-Focused Behaviors you marked for "Others":

Behaviors	You	Others
1–7		
8–14		
15–21		
Total:		

Whew! You made it through the Me-Focused list of ditchy behaviors. This exercise may have been exceedingly difficult for you. Perhaps for the first time you are realizing at a deeper level how often mistreatment happened in your family. You may have grown up in this kind of environment and never known anything different.

If you find yourself in a situation where you are physically unsafe, now is the time to seek help from a professional counselor or go to a safe house. Don't quit reading this book; take it with you. You'll discover some strategies that will help you successfully crawl out of your ditch, which is filled with powerlessness and fear that has kept you stuck for a long time.

If you discovered that you've engaged in these Ditch Behaviors, remember they were driven by an intense feeling of powerlessness and fear, and most likely you weren't even aware that's how you felt! You can start right now to shift your reactions. When you start to notice the urge to react in the negative ways as noted above, give yourself permission to take a time out and remove yourself from the situation until you have calmed down and can think of a better response.

My prayer over you:

Dear God, I pray for this dear reader. Give them courage to take action to protect themselves from the harmful actions of others—or to stop engaging in harmful actions themselves. Give them Your wisdom regarding how to proceed. Protect them in every way. Lord, if they grew up in a violent home, it's possible they have learned how to react based on the violence that was modeled for them. If this is the case, show them the way out of the patterns they have been locked into repeating. Show them the true empowerment that comes from being wholly yielded to You. In Jesus' name, amen.

Conversation starters with God:

Now it's your turn to pray. Find a quiet place. Bring a journal and pen if you enjoy writing your prayers. Above all, be prepared to listen to what God has to say to you in response. And because prayer is a conversation with someone who knows and loves you, here are a few conversations starters to get the ball rolling:

Dear God,
- Please reveal to me who to reach out to, what to say, and what my next step should be.
- What do I need to unlearn that has been hurting myself or others?
- What do You most want me to take away from today's session?

Points to ponder in group discussion or private journaling:

1. As you interacted with God, what did you hear from Him?

2. What was the biggest aha moment from this section?

3. Based on what you learned in this session, identify one action you can take that would be helpful (reminder: "noticing" counts as an action).

ME-FOCUSED BEHAVIORS: SESSION 5

We'll wrap up this chapter with a few questions designed to look at the bigger picture. We either live with someone who tends to be Me-Focused or lean toward being that way ourselves. We all stand to gain from learning new ways of responding. I hope your newfound awareness gives you a sense of hope and encouragement that things can get better. We are all capable of change when we quit trying to change others and instead turn our focus toward changing ourselves. Keep working through this study guide, and you'll discover how to do that.

1. Which of the Me-Focused Behaviors seem to happen most often in your life?

2. Do you think one ditch is better than another? Why or why not?

3. What surprised you most about this chapter?

4. What aha moments, deeper realizations, or big take-aways did you gain from this chapter?

5. What other behaviors do you think could be added to the Me-Focused list?

Remember to put anything unresolved back into your container. We'll work on finding resolution in later chapters.

> **Is there anything you would like to put in your container? If so, do it now. Feel free to make a note of what you put away.**

My prayer over you:
   Dear God, I pray that You would grant this dear reader courage to continue facing the truth and grace to accept the love and transformation You are offering. Help them to remember that behaviors coming from both ditches were learned in childhood and served a purpose when we were too young to know better. Do not allow the Accuser to use these wounds to further imprison my friend—instead, set them free. In Jesus' name, amen.

Conversation starters with God:
   Now it's your turn to pray. Find a quiet place. Bring a journal and pen if you enjoy writing your prayers. Above all, be prepared to listen to what God has to say to you in response. And because prayer is a conversation with someone who knows and loves you, here are a few conversations starters to get the ball rolling:

Dear God,
- Show me who I need to forgive. My ancestors? Parents? Myself? A spouse or a friend? Every cell in my body wants to hold onto unforgiveness, but You have said I need to forgive. Give me the power to begin that process so I can be set free.
- What do You most want me to take away from today's session?
- This journey isn't easy, but there are victories to celebrate along the way. Reveal to me something that is happening in this process that I can celebrate.

Points to ponder in group discussion or private journaling:
1. As you interacted with God, what did you hear from Him?

2. What was the biggest aha moment from this section?

3. Based on what you learned in this section, identify one action you can take that would be helpful (reminder: "noticing" counts as an action).

CHAPTER 3

WHAT DRIVES DITCH BEHAVIORS

Read or reread chapter 3 in *Unstuck*.

Main Ideas

Here is a list of the main ideas you'll find in chapter 3:
- Fear tends to run under the radar and masquerades behind other feelings.
- Beneath the surface of the "road," fear drives our reactions.
- We are not fully aware of the consequences of our behaviors on others or on ourselves.
- Fear is a spirit (2 Timothy 1:7). Being afraid does *not* mean you are possessed; it indicates you are *oppressed*.
- When unaware, we react instead of respond.
- When we stop to think about what underlies our actions, we can identify the fears that are driving them.
- Ditches are not gender specific. Our ditch depends more on how we were acculturated.
- God doesn't rank degrees of sin; people do.
- Categorization and comparison of ditchy behaviors leads to a false sense of superiority.
- When in the OF Ditch, I cannot see myself.
- When in the MF Ditch, I cannot see others.
- We tend to identify with one parent and mimic more of their actions, choosing relationships with people more like our other parent. Often, we don't recognize the similarities.

- People who experienced rejection as a child often land in the OF Ditch. This is because OFs subconsciously conclude that the secret to acceptance and love lies in passivity and being a people pleaser.
- We abandon others when trying to protect ourselves from rejection. We reject others when trying to protect ourselves from abandonment.
- OFs tend to be clueless of the impact of their actions on others.
- People with unmet emotional or physical needs feel abandoned and often land in the MF Ditch.
- Childhood abandonment causes deep-seated anger that spills into current relationships.
- Ditch Behaviors result from circumstances, significant childhood events, and dysfunctional family patterns.
- Learning about our parents' childhoods helps us to understand key factors that influenced their behaviors.
- Most of us are unaware that we could learn to communicate more effectively than we do. As a result, we don't seek help to learn better ways of relating.
- We tend to be oblivious of the patterns we repeat.
- When we objectively look at what shaped our parents' personalities and behavior patterns, identifying the baggage that got passed down to them, we become empowered to change the patterns within ourselves.
- When we live in denial, we perpetuate the problem.
- Many people influence our reactions. It's never 100 percent our fault or 100 percent the other person's fault.
- We become empowered when we identify our part and take responsibility for it.
- Our automatic default behaviors kick in when we don't know what else to do.
- Determining not to repeat what our parents did will send us to the opposite extreme unless we consciously establish a healthy alternative plan.
- It's never too late to change, even after our children have grown up.
- MFs are attracted to OFs and vice versa because of both their strengths and weaknesses.

WHAT DRIVES DITCH BEHAVIORS: SESSION 1

This chapter is divided into three sessions, though you may break it down further for both Others-Focused and Me-Focused Behaviors (1–7, 8–14, and 15–21) into three more segments. Above all, I want you to move through this at a comfortable pace. If fears start to overwhelm you, it's because they don't want to be uprooted. You can tell the fears you will lock them up, put them in a box, or give them to God for the time being until you are better equipped to deal with them one at a time. When you do it in the name of Jesus, they must obey. You may need some help to accomplish that, so don't hesitate to reach out to a qualified individual. Remember, we have power over our fears, despite their attempts to convince us otherwise!

We're going to take some time in this chapter to look at each behavior and name underlying fears to discover what is creating challenges in your life. This can be done in one of two ways:

1) Identifying and naming fears that may be driving some of your own ditchy behavior.
2) Identifying and naming fears that may be driving the ditchy behaviors of people in your life.

You choose. Either way, you will be growing in awareness of the fears that bombard you.

You'll find a place to identify and name fears in the next two sessions. But before we dive into naming these fears, I'd like us to consider some general questions:

1. When we don't know what to do or how else to react, we default to Ditch Behaviors. In what ways does it help to intentionally view those reactions as a "Ditch Behavior"?

2. How does awareness that fear drives those behaviors empower you?

3. Do you struggle more with feeling abandoned by others or feeling rejected?

4. Name a time when you felt rejected

5. Describe a situation in which you felt abandoned:

> **Is there anything you would like to put in your container? If so, do it now.
> Feel free to make a note of what you put away.**

WHAT DRIVES DITCH BEHAVIORS

My prayer over you:

Dear God, You have not given us a spirit of fear (2 Timothy 1:7). Please help this dear reader to realize that even though fears feel like feelings, they are often driven by spirits that do not want to be exposed. So please be with my friend. Provide the courage to find and name the fears that underlie their automatic reactions. I want them to gain freedom! In Jesus' name, amen.

Conversation starters with God:

Now it's your turn to pray. Find a quiet place. Bring a journal and pen if you enjoy writing your prayers. Above all, be prepared to listen to what God has to say to you in response. And because prayer is a conversation with someone who knows and loves you, here are a few conversations starters to get the ball rolling:

Dear God,
- What would You have me take away from today's session?
- In what ways have You given me power over my fears? What would You like to tell me about accessing and wielding that power?
- On a scale of one to ten, how fear-driven do You think I am?

Points to ponder in group discussion or private journaling:

1. As you interacted with God, what did you hear from Him?

2. What was the biggest aha moment from this section?

3. Based on what you learned in this session, identify one action you can take that would be helpful.

WHAT DRIVES DITCH BEHAVIORS: SESSION 2

Remember, there are no wrong answers as you progress through this study guide. If you're doing this study in a group, you may hear people identify and name a wide variety of fears, which may help you recognize fears that didn't come up for you even though you may have experienced them.

Ironically, there's power in expressing our fears. This, of course, was not the message many of us received growing up. Instead, people—especially boys and men—have been ridiculed, taunted, or bullied for showing or expressing fear. If this is your story, this chapter may feel challenging at times, in which case I encourage you to use the container exercise as needed—and, most importantly, press on.

Throughout our lives we will continue to be bombarded with valid fears when faced with challenges and trials. Identifying and naming our fears helps diminish their control and even helps us overcome their influence over our lives.

At this point, I'm not asking you to go beyond simply naming your fears. We'll refer back to this chapter when we discuss what to do about fear in chapter 16.

Following, you'll find a list of common Others-Focused Ditch Behaviors. As you look at each one, recall a time when you demonstrated that behavior yourself or observed that behavior in someone else. What fears might have been fueling your actions? Identify and write down as many as you can. You may wish to refer to the examples given in the book or to the work you did in chapter one.

Fears Driving Others-Focused Behaviors:

For each of the following, name as many fears as you can that underlie or drive these behaviors:

1. People Pleasing:

2. Default Answer *Yes*:

3. Readily Giving up What I Want:

4. Difficulty Making Decisions:

5. Walking on Eggshells:

6. Difficulty Expressing Feelings or Opinions:

7. Codependence:

8. Avoiding:

9. Blaming:

10. Being Passive:

11. Feeling Obligated:

12. Being Resentful:

13. Being Sarcastic:

14. Being Critical and/or Gossipy:

15. Nursing Hurts:

16. Being Passive-Aggressive:

17. Withdrawing:

18. Shutting Down:

19. Experiencing Chaos:

20. Playing the Victim:

21. Wanting to Self-Harm:

> **Is there anything you would like to put in your container? If so, do it now. Feel free to make a note of what you put away.**

My prayer over you:

*Dear God, I pray for this dear reader as they begin to explore the role that fear has played in their life. I invite Your presence into the process. I think of the words of the psalmist, who wrote, "I sought the L*ORD*, and he answered me and delivered me from all my fears" (Psalm 34:4). Answer the prayers of this reader, Father, and bring freedom and deliverance into their life. In Jesus' name, amen.*

Conversation starters with God:

Now it's your turn to pray. Find a quiet place. Bring a journal and pen if you enjoy writing your prayers. Above all, be prepared to listen to what God has to say to you in response. And because prayer is a conversation with someone who knows and loves you, here are a few conversations starters to get the ball rolling:

Dear God,
- What do You most want for me to take away from today's session?
- Have I missed anything in doing the above exercise that You would like me to go back and revisit? Are there other memories or situations You want to bring to my mind?
- The psalmist sought You, and You delivered him from his fears. How would You like for me to seek You?

Points to ponder in group discussion or private journaling:
1. As you interacted with God, what did you hear from Him?

2. What was the biggest aha moment from this section?

3. Based on what you learned in this session, identify one action you can take that would be helpful.

WHAT DRIVES DITCH BEHAVIORS: SESSION 3

Below you'll find a list of common Me-Focused Ditch Behaviors. As you look at each one, recall a time you demonstrated that behavior yourself or observed it in someone else. What fears might have been fueling that action? Identify and write down as many as you can. You may wish to refer to the examples given in the book or to the work you did in chapter one.

Fears Driving Me-Focused Behaviors:

For each of the following, name as many fears as you can think of that underlie or drive these behaviors:

1. Selfishness:

2. Default Answer *No*:

3. Perfectionism:

4. Need to Be Right:

5. Difficulty Seeing Others' Perspectives:

6. Difficulty Expressing Thoughts and Feelings or Opinions:

7. Demanding:

8. Manipulating:

9. Criticizing:

10. Controlling:

11. Vocal About Feelings and Wants:

12. High Expectations:

13. Disappointed in Others:

14. Angry:

15. Demeaning:

16. Threatening:

17. Yelling:

18. Attacking/Accusing:

19. Rigid:

20. Becoming Addicted:

21. Harming Others:

> **Is there anything you would like to put in your container? If so, do it now. Feel free to make a note of what you put away.**

Let's revisit the words of the apostle Paul in 2 Timothy 1:7: "For God has not given us a spirit of fear, but of power and of love and of a sound mind."

There are two parts to that sentence. I think of them as opposite ends of a continuum. Fear sits on one side; power, love, and a sound mind—which we often call *sanity*—sits on the other side.

If we have a spirit of fear, it follows that we are robbed of having power, love, and a sound mind. In the extreme, this leads to insanity. And if we are walking in power, love, and sound thinking, it is unlikely that we are living in fear.

I'm not saying these opposites are mutually exclusive, or that we will never find ourselves in the middle of the continuum, experiencing some of both. However, I will say that we will be unable to fully experience all that God has for us when we allow our fears to roam about undetected and unchecked.

Where are you on this continuum today?

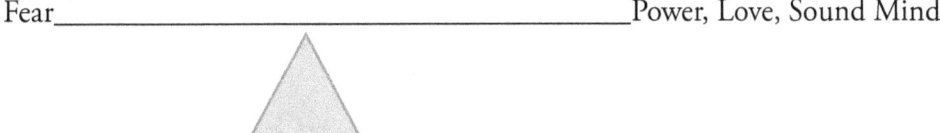

Fear_____Power, Love, Sound Mind

Because we will be attacked by fears from time to time throughout our lives, we can gauge our progress, and assess whenever we are feeling fearful, by assessing where we are on the continuum.

My prayer over you:

Dear God, I pray for this dear reader as they learn how to identify the hidden fears impacting their life. Help them to learn this skill well, practicing it now and in the future, so they can fully embrace the power, love, and sanity You long to give them. In Jesus' name, amen.

Conversation starters with God:

Now it's your turn to pray. Find a quiet place. Bring a journal and pen if you enjoy writing your prayers. Above all, be prepared to listen to what God has to say to you in response. And because prayer is a conversation with someone who knows and loves you, here are a few conversations starters to get the ball rolling:

Dear God,
- What do You most want for me to take away from today's session?
- Have I missed anything in doing the above exercise that You would like me to go back and revisit? Are there other memories or situations You want to bring to my mind?
- Paul wrote to Timothy that You have not given us a spirit of fear. Will You remind me of this verse over the next few days?

Points to ponder in group discussion or private journaling:

1. As you interacted with God, what did you hear from Him?

2. What was the biggest aha moment from this section?

3. Based on what you learned in this session, identify one action you can take that would be helpful to eliminate.

WHAT DRIVES DITCH BEHAVIORS: SESSION 4

It's so refreshing to discover that we can climb out of the murky haze of fear that keeps us in the ditch and step out into the clear light of day onto the road!

But how did we get in the ditch in the first place?

There are three factors we need to consider: family of origin, circumstances beyond our control, and personal choices.

Let's take a look at each:

A. Your Family of Origin

1. Were you born in a ditch? In other words, was your family of origin dysfunctional in some way? Yes____ No____

2. Did you witness extreme behaviors in your parents? And by parents, I mean primary caretakers when you were a child, who may include grandparents, stepparents, or other caregivers. If so, what did you observe?

3. Which of your parents, stepparents, or other caretakers tended toward being Others-Focused?

4. Which of your parents, stepparents, or other caretakers tended toward being Me-Focused?

5. Which parent, stepparent, or caretaker are you most like?

6. What is your Ditch of Choice (DOC)?

B. Circumstances Beyond Your Control

Let's examine circumstances beyond your control that may have pushed you into the ditch. Possibilities include abuse, a natural disaster, fire, war, 9/11, COVID-19, death, disability, prison, murder, suicide, illness, loss of job or home, or poverty. Also consider anything you found challenging when you were growing up, such as moving, parents divorcing, remarriage of a parent, family discord, loss of a friend, or bullying.

1. What circumstances in your life left an indelible mark on you as you were growing up that made you feel like you got pushed into a ditch?

2. What situations in childhood did you experience that were especially hard for you?

C. Personal Choices

1. What mistakes have you made that you have attempted to rationalize, justify, or minimize?

2. What ditchy things have you done that have impacted your life, bearing consequences you didn't anticipate or consider?

3. What significant events have impacted your behaviors in a negative way?

4. Which ditches do you think other family members tend to favor? (Name the person(s) and the ditch you think is their DOC.)

Is there anything you would like to put in your container? If so, do it now. Feel free to make a note of what you put away.

We talked about family of origin, but I'd like to expand our look at family to include our ancestors. How is this helpful? Let me give you an example from my life. Learning what my dad went through as a child and young adult gave me a lot more compassion for him and helped me understand why he carried the anger he did. It didn't excuse his behavior, but it did drive home for me the powerful role that forgiveness plays in our ability to crawl out of the ditch. (Forgiveness makes it possible to experience peace in our lives, despite our wounding!)

Before you start the following exercise, let me acknowledge that it's possible your parents seldom talked about what their childhoods were like. If so, you may not know about the good times they had, the struggles they faced, or the difficulties they navigated. If this describes you, consider having a conversation with your parents (if they are still alive), siblings, or other relatives willing to share stories. Start by asking about the good memories—they are always easier to talk about!

1. What are some significant events that happened in your dad's childhood?

2. What are some significant events that happened in your mom's childhood?

Our family history also plays a significant role. What our ancestors experienced impacted them, it influenced our parents, and then some of it landed on us, thus spreading to future generations. Our parents' experiences shaped their world view, education level, financial status, vocation, belief systems, and parenting styles. Abuses also got passed down generationally. Most of the time it didn't start with our parents, or their parents either!

We are directly influenced today by what happened in the past, though I never thought of that connection until later in life. Looking at the pivotal events in the lives of our forefathers adds perspective to why your parents turned out the way they did and how they treated you. What events shaped their lives? Wealth, poverty, oppression, separation from family, suicide, murder, disabilities, illness, abuse, a major move, famine, war, death?

For example, my great-grandfather on my dad's side committed suicide in the late 1800s when my grandmother was nine years old, leaving her with eight siblings, ranging from six months to age fifteen to be raised by a widow. This story was never discussed in our family while I was growing up, and I only learned about it when I was in my thirties. However, it had a major impact on my grandmother and my dad; therefore, some of the fallout landed on us kids. It affected my father's family's self-esteem, financial situation, social status, familial roles, and relationships.

1. When you think of your dad's father (your grandfather), what do you know about his story?

2. Regarding your dad's mother (your grandmother), what do you know about her story?

3. When you think of your mom's father (your grandfather), what do you know about his story?

4. Regarding your mom's mother (your grandmother), what do you know about her story?

5. When you think about your extended family, what stories of success or hardship come to mind?

As you completed this exercise, the stories and memories that surfaced probably ranged from happy, hilarious, and poignant to uncomfortable, unhappy, and painful—and everything in between.

This is to be expected. From the time Adam and Eve partook of the Tree of Knowledge of Good and Evil, life has been a mix of both good and bad. If this section was particularly difficult for you, seek the help of a therapist to assist you in processing the questions and your feelings about the experience. Addressing these feelings and experiences will set you free from the negativity and pain that has kept you trapped and stuck.

My prayer over you:

Dear God, thank You for revealing things in the life of this dear reader that may be keeping them stuck. As You see fit, help them to find the right person(s) to help them work through any wounds that need to be further addressed so they can be set free. In Jesus' name, amen.

Conversation starters with God:

Now it's your turn to pray. Find a quiet place. Bring a journal and pen if you enjoy writing your prayers. Above all, be prepared to listen to what God has to say to you in response. And because prayer is a conversation with someone who knows and loves you, here are a few conversations starters to get the ball rolling:

Dear God,
- What do You most want for me to take away from today's session?
- Are there past generational events in my family that are holding me back in this current time? Would You reveal these to me so I can be set free?
- Am I harboring unforgiveness that is negatively affecting me? If so, can You reveal to me strongholds of unforgiveness that You and I may need to address together?

Points to ponder in group discussion or private journaling:

1. As you interacted with God, what did you hear from Him?

2. What was the biggest aha moment from this section?

3. Based on what you learned in this session, identify one action you can take that would be helpful.

CHAPTER 4

SWITCHING DITCHES

Read or reread chapter 4 in *Unstuck*.

Main Ideas

Here is a list of the main ideas you'll find in chapter 4:
- When our tactics in one ditch fail to be successful, we switch to the other extreme.
- The way we behave in the opposite ditch is just different enough that no one picks up on what's happening.
- Most of the time, when I switch ditches, my partner is propelled to the other ditch in an attempt to maintain equilibrium.
- The way Ditch Behaviors manifest (with whom, what's happening, the frequency in which a behavior occurs, and the topic) all influence our ditch-switching tendencies.
- We have a DOC (Ditch of Choice), which is our default mode of reacting.
- Depending on the topic, this transfer can happen multiple times in one interchange.
- We may be MF in one relationship and OF in another.
- The greatest fear for an OF is rejection, which they attempt to sidestep by abandoning.
- The greatest fear of a MF is abandonment, which they attempt to avoid by rejecting.
- Because we switch ditches, we also switch between fear of abandonment and fear of rejection.

- Both OFs and MFs unknowingly pull into their lives what they are trying to avoid by their ditchy behaviors.
- When an OF steps out of the ditch, the most difficult truth to accept is "*I allowed that.*"
- When a MF steps out of the ditch, the most difficult truth to accept is "*I did that.*"

SWITCHING DITCHES: SESSION 1

I bet you didn't see this coming.

The shocking truth is that we switch ditches when our default behaviors in our DOC (Ditch of Choice) no longer serve us. That means if you lean toward Others-Focused Ditch Behaviors, you're not above resorting to Me-Focused Ditch Behaviors (which you probably abhor) when you feel afraid and powerless.

And vice versa.

My DOC is Others-Focused. Discovering that I switch to the Me-Focused Ditch revolutionized how I saw relationships! I had so strongly identified with being the "martyr" or "victim" that it was mind-blowing to realize I was *also* guilty of Me-Focused Ditch Behaviors, such as selfishness, anger, and attacking others.

This revelation leveled the playing field and knocked me right off my self-righteous high horse. Even though my spouse did hurtful things to me that I assured myself I would never have done to him, I realized I treated him in unhealthy ways too. When I was being aggressive or hurtful, it looked different on the surface than the way my spouse manifested those behaviors, but it wasn't so different after all. For example, I might not retaliate against him; instead, I'd lash out against myself or someone else (especially someone weaker or smaller than me).

The movie *Three Billboards Outside Ebbing, Missouri* illustrates powerfully how the main character switches ditches from victim to attacker.

Everyone does this. Though not everyone realizes they do this.

Let's take a look at this dynamic in your life.

1. How does the idea that you can switch ditches affect you?

   What signs of ditch-switching can you identify in your life?

2. On what topics do you tend to go to the opposite extreme?

3. On which issues does it feel like the only solution is win-lose (one gets his/her desires met and the other one doesn't)?

Now let's go back to your answers from the Others-Focused Ditch in chapter 1. I want you to take a second look at those behaviors. Here we will look for reactions that you did not identify in yourself in chapters 1 and 2. Spend some time thinking and note incidences in which you may have exhibited a specific Ditch Behavior.

With whom did you respond that way? Note the topic if possible. Also, for those behaviors in chapters 1 and 2 that you noticed in yourself but not in others, think of an example of how that behavior appeared in someone else.

As you do this, you'll begin to see how we mirror one another even though *how* these behaviors manifest and the *proportion* to which we engage these actions may be significantly different. For example, he seems angry 80 percent of the time when she exhibits anger 20 percent of the time. She might automatically say yes 90 percent of the time, yet he says yes 10 percent of the time.

If you noted the behavior in chapter 1 as something you do, then for this exercise think of an example when your partner did this. Likewise, if in chapter 1 you noticed this in someone else, then in this chapter think of a time you have done this.

For each of the following, check whether you are answering for yourself or the other person, then give an example.

Others-Focused Ditch Behaviors:

1. **People Pleasing**
   You _____
   Other Person _____
   Give an example:

2. **Default Answer** *Yes*
   You _____
   Other Person _____
   On what topics?

3. **Readily Giving Up What I Want**
   You _____
   Other Person _____
   Share a recent example:

4. **Difficulty Making Decisions**
   You _____
   Other Person _____
   On which topics is decision-making difficult?

5. **Walking on Eggshells**
   You _____
   Other Person _____
   What are the eggshell topics?

6. **Difficulty Expressing Feelings or Opinions**
   You _____
   Other Person _____
   With what topics does this occur?

7. **Avoiding**
   You _____
   Other Person _____
   What topics seem the most difficult to discuss?

**Is there anything you would like to put in your container? If so, do it now.
Feel free to make a note of what you put away.**

My prayer over you:

Dear God, it's so easy to judge others. I pray for this dear reader as they realize they have engaged in some of the very behaviors they may have judged harshly in others. In this process, allow them to adopt a spirit of grace toward themselves—and toward others as well. In Jesus' name, amen.

Conversation starters with God:

Now it's your turn to pray. Find a quiet place. Bring a journal and pen if you enjoy writing your prayers. Above all, be prepared to listen to what God has to say to you in response. And because prayer is a conversation with someone who knows and loves you, here are a few conversations starters to get the ball rolling:

Dear God,
- What do You most want for me to take away from today's session?
- Help me to grasp the idea of "switching ditches," and show me how I am hurting others in ways I have yet to acknowledge.
- Remove from me any shame or accusations I might be tempted to hurl at myself.
- Surround me in Your grace. Help me to have grace for myself. How do You see me, Father? Show me that too.

Points to ponder in group discussion or private journaling:

1. As you interacted with God, what did you hear from Him?

2. What was the biggest aha moment from this section?

3. Based on what you learned in this session, identify one action you can take that would be helpful.

SWITCHING DITCHES: SESSION 2

Today we will look at the middle seven Others-Focused Ditch Behaviors: numbers 8–14. We continue our journey of noticing. If you noted the behavior in chapter 1 as something you do, then for this exercise think of an example when your counterpart did this. Likewise, if in chapter 1 you noticed this in someone else, then in this chapter think of a time you have done this. For each of the following, check whether you are answering for yourself or the other person, then give an example.

8. Codependence (trying to save or "fix" others in order to feel needed; putting others' needs before your own")
You _____
Other Person _____
Example:

9. Blaming
You _____
Other Person _____
Example:

10. Being Passive
You _____
Other Person _____
Example:

11. Feeling Obligated
You _____
Other Person _____
Example:

12. Being Resentful
You _____
Other Person _____
Share an experience:

13. Being Sarcastic
You _____
Other Person _____
Provide an illustration:

14. Being Critical and/or Gossipy
You _____
Other Person _____
What kinds of critical remarks?

> **Is there anything you would like to put in your container? If so, do it now. Feel free to make a note of what you put away.**

I remember when I was blind to seeing these behaviors in either myself or my spouse. Once I became aware of them, I could see them everywhere! Has that been your experience too? Awareness is indeed the first step of change.

My prayer over you:

Dear God, I pray for this dear reader as You open their eyes to unhealthy behavior in themselves and others. Please uplift and encourage them in this process. Impart a sense of joyful anticipation. Remind my friend that this exercise, while temporarily painful, provides an opportunity for You to shine, and that freedom is around the corner. In Jesus' name, amen.

Conversation starters with God:

Now it's your turn to pray. Find a quiet place. Bring a journal and pen if you enjoy writing your prayers. Above all, be prepared to listen to what God has to say to you in response. And because prayer is a conversation with someone who knows and loves you, here are a few conversations starters to get the ball rolling:

Dear God,
- What do You most want for me to take away from today's session?
- The psalmist says in Psalm 145:18 that you are near to all who call on You in truth. As I journey out of denial and into greater truth about

behaviors holding me back, please draw near to me. Will you help me feel Your presence right now?
- Please give me a glimpse of the freedom You have for me. What do You want to show me?

Points to ponder in group discussion or private journaling:

1. As you interacted with God, what did you hear from Him?

2. What was the biggest aha moment from this section?

3. Based on what you learned in this session, identify one action you can take that would be helpful.

SWITCHING DITCHES: SESSION 3

We continue our exploration of the Ditch Behaviors from the viewpoint of having switched ditches. Today, we will look at the last seven Others-Focused Ditch Behaviors: numbers 15–21. If you noted the behavior in chapter 1 as something you do, for this exercise, think of an example when your counterpart did this. Likewise, if in chapter 1 you noticed this in someone else, then in this chapter, think of a time you have done this.

For each of the following, check whether you are answering for yourself or for the other person, then give an example.

15. Nursing Hurts
You _____
Other Person _____
Provide an example:

16. Being Passive-Aggressive
You _____
Other Person _____
Provide an example of passive-aggressive behavior you have experienced:

17. Withdrawing
You _____
Other Person _____
What topics are involved when withdrawing happens?

18. Shutting down
You _____
Other Person _____
Example:

19. Experiencing Chaos
You _____
Other Person _____
Provide an example of chaos in your life:

20. Playing the Victim
You _____
Other Person _____
What does playing the victim look like?

21. Wanting to Self-Harm
You _____
Other Person _____
What kind of self-harm have you inflicted upon yourself?

> **Is there anything you would like to put in your container? If so, do it now. Feel free to make a note of what you put away.**

Now you have a clearer picture of how everyone engages in Others-Focused Ditch Behaviors from time to time. The biggest difference is *how* and the *frequency*. Remember, we're not in the ditch all the time, only when we don't know how to balance our wishes with those of another. That's when we find ourselves, the other, or both of us in the ditch. Now we can begin our journey to freedom. After all, a map can only help us reach a new destination when we know where we are starting from.

My prayer over you:

Dear God, Thank You for opening my dear reader's eyes to a deeper understanding of Matthew 7:3. You talk about having a plank in my eye when others have a speck in theirs, yet it seems just the opposite! Please remove the planks! In Jesus' name, amen.

Conversation starters with God:

Now it's your turn to pray. Find a quiet place. Bring a journal and pen if you enjoy writing your prayers. Above all, be prepared to listen to what God has to say to you in response. And because prayer is a conversation with someone who knows and loves you, here are a few conversations starters to get the ball rolling:

Dear God,
- What do You most want for me to take away from today's session?
- In some ways it helps to know that we all switch ditches, and in some ways it's a little overwhelming. Is it really possible to stop resorting to these extreme, unhealthy behaviors? What are Your thoughts on this?
- Why is this so difficult? Is it because I can't do it on my own and challenges like this are meant to encourage me to lean on You? In what areas would You like me to depend on You more?

Points to ponder in group discussion or private journaling:

1. As you interacted with God, what did you hear from Him?

2. What was the biggest aha moment from this section?

3. Based on what you learned in this session, identify one action you can take that would be helpful.

SWITCHING DITCHES: SESSION 4

Today we examine where Me-Focused Ditch Behaviors appear in the lives of others or in our lives that we may not have noticed before. Go back to your answers from chapter 2, the Me-Focused Ditch. Take another look at the behaviors you noticed in others but not yourself, or noticed in yourself but not in others.

If you noted the behavior in chapter 2 as something you do, then for this exercise, think of an example when your counterpart did this. Likewise, if in chapter 2 you noticed this in someone else, then in this chapter think of a time you have done this.

For each of the following, check whether you are answering for yourself or the other person, then give an example.

1. Selfish
You ____
Other Person _____
What did that look like?

2. Default Answer *No*
You ____
Other Person _____
What topics tend to get a no response?

3. Perfectionism
You _____
Other Person _____
In what area(s) is perfectionism important?

4. Need to Be Right
You _____
Other Person _____
Provide an example of when being right took precedence:

5. Difficulty Seeing Others' Perspectives
You _____
Other Person _____
Describe a situation where this happened:

6. Demanding
You _____
Other Person _____
Give an example:

7. Manipulative
You _____
Other Person _____
What does manipulation look like in your behaviors? In the behavior of others?

> **Is there anything you would like to put in your container? If so, do it now. Feel free to make a note of what you put away.**

Were you surprised to discover how these behaviors show up in the actions of others as well as in your own actions? I certainly was surprised when I began to see this in my own life. I'm so glad you're on this journey with me!

My prayer over you:

Dear God, You knew what You were talking about when You told us to take the plank out of our own eyes before telling someone else to take the speck out of theirs! (Matthew 7:3). Why is it so easy to see unhealthy behavior in others but not in ourselves? I pray for my dear reader as they continue on their journey toward healing and freedom. Bring clarity and joy to this process. In Jesus' name, amen.

Conversation starters with God:

Now it's your turn to pray. Find a quiet place. Bring a journal and pen if you enjoy writing your prayers. Above all, be prepared to listen to what God has to say to you in response. And because prayer is a conversation with someone who knows and loves you, here are a few conversations starters to get the ball rolling:

Dear God,
- What do You most want for me to take away from today's session?
- Help me to hear Your voice with greater clarity. Help me to tune out distractions (including my own distracting thoughts) and really listen to You now. What are You saying to me today?
- I want to root out the unhealthy stuff I'm doing. I'm tired of living in denial. I'm ready to bring things into the light so they will lose their power over me. At the same time, You know what I'd love right now? I'd love to know what You see in me that makes You smile. What about me brings You joy?

Points to ponder in group discussion or private journaling:

1. As you interacted with God, what did you hear from Him?

2. What was the biggest aha moment from this section?

3. Based on what you learned in this session, identify one action you can take that would be helpful.

SWITCHING DITCHES: SESSION 5

We continue our exploration of how and where Me-Focused Ditch Behaviors appear. If you noted the behavior in chapter 2 as something you do, for this exercise, think of an example when your counterpart did this. Likewise, if in chapter 2 you noticed this in someone else, then in this session, think of a time you have acted this way.

For each of the following, check whether you are answering for yourself or for the other person, then give an example.

8. Criticizing
You _____
Other Person _____
What is a specific area where you are critical or feel criticized?

9. Controlling
You _____
Other Person _____
Provide an example of a controlling behavior:

10. Vocal about Feelings and Wants
You _____
Other Person _____
On what topics?

11. High Expectations (school, work, home, appearance, actions, etc.)
You _____
Other Person _____
Example:

12. Disappointment
You _____
Other Person _____
Provide an illustration of disappointment:

13. Angry
You _____
Other Person _____
Furnish an example:

14. Demeaning
You _____
Other Person _____
Offer an example of demeaning behavior:

> **Is there anything you would like to put in your container? If so, do it now. Feel free to make a note of what you put away.**

Recognizing these behaviors in ourselves and others helps us see how we can improve our lives. We gain power to change when we see what we are doing and how we are triggered by the actions of others. These types of reactions have been going on and have been passed down for generations. Awareness of our Ditch Behaviors helps us become game changers. We create a better world starting at home.

My prayer over you:
Dear God, I pray for this dear reader, and thank You for raising their awareness of things that have been happening on autopilot for much of their life. Thank You for freeing them from strongholds they did not even know were there. Thank You for showing them a better way to live. In Jesus' name, amen.

Conversation starters with God:
Now it's your turn to pray. Find a quiet place. Bring a journal and pen if you enjoy writing your prayers. Above all, be prepared to listen to what God has to say to you in response. And because prayer is a conversation with someone who knows and loves you, here are a few conversations starters to get the ball rolling:

Dear God,
- What do You most want for me to take away from today's session?
- I realize that many of the unhealthy behaviors I embraced were mod-

eled for me by other people—parents and other role models—in my life. Is there anything I need to be doing today in these relationships? Forgiving someone? Setting better boundaries? Asking for forgiveness?
- Help me forgive myself for how I have reacted to other people's unhealthy behaviors and for how I have engaged in unhealthy behaviors myself. What do I need to forgive myself for?

Points to ponder in group discussion or private journaling:
1. As you interacted with God, what did you hear from Him?

2. What was the biggest aha moment from this section?

3. Based on what you learned in this session, identify one action you can take that would be helpful.

SWITCHING DITCHES: SESSION 6

This is the last session about switching ditches. Next, we will explore how we react when we find ourselves in situations that are out of control, leaving us feeling powerless. If you noted the behavior in chapter 2 as something you do, then for this exercise think of an example when your counterpart did this. Likewise, if in chapter 2 you noticed this in someone else, then in this session think of a time you have acted this way.

None of us are proud of these moments. In fact, we can live with shame—or blocked or numbed emotions—as a result of how we've been treated or how we've reacted in the past.

The good news is that there is freedom to be gained by confessing what we have done and experienced. James 5:16 (NIV) tells us: "Therefore confess your sins to each other and pray for each other so that you may be healed. The prayer of a righteous person is powerful and effective." There's power in confession!

It's important that we not judge ourselves or others because we're all guilty at some level.

For each of the following, check whether you are answering for yourself or for the other person, then give an example.

15. Threatening
You _____
Other Person _____

Parents, leaders, authorities, teachers, and governments commonly use threats to coerce others into compliance. During COVID-19 in 2020 and 2021, most stores threatened to or refused entry unless customers used face masks. Punishment, deprivation, or the possibility of other negative consequences are leveraged to get people to behave how others want them to behave. Often, the motivation is positive, but the methods used could be improved.

Think of a situation in which a threat was involved:

16. Yelling
You _____
Other Person _____
Name an example in which yelling occurred:

17. Attacking/Accusing
You _____
Other Person _____
An attack is telling someone else what they should do, ought to do, have done, or would have done themselves. An accusation is telling someone that they did something wrong.
Provide an example of this:

18. Rigid
You _____
Other Person _____
Being rigid is when you have strict ways of doing something, coupled with the unwillingness to consider anyone else's input.
Give an example of rigidity:

19. Addict
You _____
Other Person _____
I would venture to bet that at some level we all turn to something when feeling anxious, whether it's TV, a game, work, food, exercise, social media, drugs, alcohol,

relationships, or sex. What automatic habits to ease anxiety or numb out do you commonly use?

20. Physical Attacks
You _____
Other Person _____
Did a physical attack happen to you during childhood or in your adult life? If yes, provide an example:

21. Harming Others
You _____
Other Person _____
While this is similar to physical attacks, there are lots of ways harm occurs without physically attacking. This happens through words or actions, saying mean and hurtful things, through shaming, and by damaging or destroying property or one's reputation.
Provide an example:

CHAPTER 5

EVERYONE IS AFRAID

Read or reread chapter 5 in *Unstuck*.

Main Ideas

Here is a list of the main ideas you'll find in chapter 5:
- We tend to be quick to deny the fear we experience.
- Often, the fear driving anger, rage, hurt, and stress goes undetected.
- In our culture, men are taught to hide or deny fear, which then leaks out (or explodes) as anger.
- Fear exists on a continuum from concern to sheer terror.
- Acknowledging and naming fear helps us determine which strategies to use to overcome it.
- Suppressed fear erupts as anger and rage.
- There are many ways to clear out fears once identified.
- Secondary emotions of anger include frustration, guilt, insecurity, inferiority, sadness, grief, or trauma—under all of that is fear.
- Rage is uncontrollable anger.
- Hurt is bottled up anger turned inward against self.
- Stress is driven by fear.
- Often fear comes from not knowing how to trust God with that area of our lives.
- God can help us overcome fear.

EVERYONE IS AFRAID: SESSION 1

In this chapter we look "under the hood" of our emotions, specifically examining fears in hiding. Most commonly, we can find fears lurking beneath anger, rage, hurt, and stress.

At one time I had printed a list of over four hundred named phobias from a worldwide web search. If you are curious, just do an Internet search on phobias, and you'll have a plethora of lists to examine. For each area in our lives in which a phobia exists, we are restricted and not free to live fully. For example, a fear of spiders might keep us from going into caves or basements. A fear of birds will keep us from the beach where sea gulls congregate, or city parks where pigeons gather. A fear of dogs will keep us from venturing out in our neighborhoods. A fear of flying will rob us of the joy of exploring the world. A fear of germs or getting COVID-19 will keep us locked up and isolated at home.

Most fears, of course, are founded on an element of truth. Spiders *can* be poisonous; a bird *might* get too close; dogs *may* attack; we *could* experience turbulence while flying; and some planes *have* crashed. Some people *have* gotten sick from germs, and COVID-19 *has* proven deadly for some.

We are challenged to discover a way to navigate life despite the potential dangers. A few options do exist though:

1. We can avoid any potential of running into a situation in which we may meet our fears face-to-face. That means avoiding any place a spider might lurk, a bird might fly, a dog could be on the loose, an airplane might lift off the ground, or a human might carry a virus.
2. Another approach requires facing that fear, calculating the risks, and determining what we need to do to live wise but free.
3. A third option involves evaluating each situation that comes along, then determining the best course of action based on those circumstances.

The third option requires more emotional energy than the first two. Therefore, as a society we default to mandates everyone must follow whether or not they are practical, helpful, or make sense.

The basis of our intense fears rests in some bad experience in our past, which we may or may not remember. Often the experience that brought on the fear is long forgotten. Or you might have inherited the fear. You don't have to know when or how it started, but learning how to let it go will free you to live more fully. Most people opt to live with the phobia because it seems too scary (another fear supporting the existence of the phobia) to address it.

Fears run in packs like wolves. They reinforce one another and make it harder for us to overcome them. But, just like pulling back the curtain of the Wizard of Oz to discover he's just a man, pulling back the shroud hiding our fears causes them to shrink too.

What fears or phobias do you live with daily—or that recur in similar situations—that just seem to be part of who you are? Do you feel unsafe? Worried about finances? Concerned about relationships? Tenuous about job security? Longing to have what you want? Stuck with some compulsive behavior?

The more you can recognize the fears driving your actions, the more you will feel empowered to do something about them. Remember, it's a process, and the fears won't all go away at once. Taking time now to name them will prepare you for chapter 16. There, we will apply strategies to overcome these fears.

Now let's shift our focus to the fears hiding beneath anger. This can be difficult because our culture taught us to disconnect our fear feelings from anger. So what's behind your anger?

You might want to break it down further to get in touch with the fears. First, name what it is and then ponder what fear(s) could be underlying. It might help to enlist the perspective of someone close to you to help you put words to your internal experience. Perhaps the following questions will help.

1a. What do you feel frustrated about (job, home, kids, goals, finances, etc.)?

1b. What could be some of the underlying fears?

2a. What do you feel guilty about?

2b. What are you afraid will happen because of what you feel guilty about?

3a. What insecurities or inferiorities surface?

3b. What lies beneath? Example: I'm afraid I'm not (good, pretty, educated, or smart) enough.

4a. What sadness, grief, or regret do you carry with you?

4b. What could some of the underlying fears be, related to those feelings?

5a. What traumas, bad experiences, abuses, losses, or accidents haunt you?

5b. What fears were established because of those experiences?

6a. With whom do you tend to express anger most frequently? (kids, coworkers, spouse, parents, siblings?)

6b. How does your anger typically manifest (yelling, slamming doors, throwing things, shutting down)?

Some of these things may be deep-seated, so you may benefit from the assistance of a professional coach or counselor to help you work through them in a way that's not too overwhelming to handle.

> **Is there anything you would like to put in your container? If so, do it now. Feel free to make a note of what you put away.**

My prayer over you:
Dear God, I pray for this dear reader as they examine anger, what has fueled it, and how it has manifested and affected relationships. Please give this individual compassion for themselves and those around them. Help them to forgive the people who caused the anger and to forgive themselves for reacting in anger. In Jesus' name, amen.

Conversation starters with God:
Now it's your turn to pray. Find a quiet place. Bring a journal and pen if you enjoy writing your prayers. Above all, be prepared to listen to what God has to say to you in response. And because prayer is a conversation with someone who knows and loves you, here are a few conversations starters to get the ball rolling:

Dear God,
- What do You most want for me to learn from today's session?
- Are there any fears that have remained hidden? If yes, what are they?
- Show me how to have compassion on myself for the ways I've acted in the past.

Points to ponder in group discussion or private journaling:

1. As you interacted with God, what did you hear from Him?

2. What was the biggest aha moment from this section?

3. Based on what you learned in this session, identify one action you can take that would be helpful.

EVERYONE IS AFRAID: SESSION 2

In this session we examine fears underlying rage, hurt and stress.

A. Amped-up anger and intense feelings of powerlessness leak out sideways as rage, though we may remain unaware of the feeling of powerlessness. There are two distinct characteristics to rage:

1. Becoming easily triggered by minor things, such as someone pulling in front of us on the road. A comment made by someone else rubs us the wrong way. The tone of someone's voice, or a possibly phrase can set us off. What are some things that trigger your rage?

2. The reaction is disproportionate to the trigger that set us off. It's a rage response when we overreact. Most of the time we are not aware of how we overreacted until after we have calmed down. In what ways have you overreacted in the past?

B. Coins have a different image on each side, but it's still one coin. When we flip a coin, we know it's the same coin whether heads or tails show up. Likewise, the flipside of anger is hurt. When we feel angry, our tendency is to lash out at others. When experiencing hurt, we turn that inward toward ourselves. Underneath that emotional pain, fear is lurking. Let's see if we can discover what those fears might be.

1. In what ways do you feel injured?

1a. Physical hurt?

1b. What did you tell yourself about that injury or the person who hurt you?

2a. Emotional? (feeling invalidated, unheard, unloved, etc.)

2b. As a result of what happened, what did you conclude about yourself, your self-worth, your potential, your ability to be loved?

3a. Mental? (feeling put down, embarrassed, rejected, abandoned)

3b. As a result of what happened, what did you conclude about who you are, your self-worth, your potential, your ability to be loved?

C. The last big rock under which fears hide is stress. The easiest way to identify the fears hiding there is to list all the things you feel stressed about, such as kids, finances, work, school, illness, relationships, etc.

1. What are you stressed about?

2. As you look at each item that triggers your stress, consider, "What am I afraid will happen (or will not happen)?"

We will revisit the answers to these questions when we get to chapter 16. Then we'll figure out the best strategies for addressing the fears. Until then, pat yourself on the back. Digging up hidden fears takes work, and it's just their nature to scare you!

Is there anything you would like to put in your container? If so, do it now. Feel free to make a note of what you put away.

My prayer over you:

Dear God, I pray for this dear reader as they begin to see preprogrammed, automatic behavior defaults. Thank You for raising awareness, for bringing the root of these behaviors—which is fear—into the light. In Jesus' name, amen.

Conversation starters with God:

Now it's your turn to pray. Find a quiet place. Bring a journal and pen if you enjoy writing your prayers. Above all, be prepared to listen to what God has to say to you in response. And because prayer is a conversation with someone who knows and loves you, here are a few conversations starters to get the ball rolling:

Dear God,
- What do You most want for me to take away from today's session?
- What fear or fears do You want me to address first in this journey toward becoming free of rage or hurt?
- Where do You want me to start in reducing stress in my life?
- Have I been nursing hurts? Please show me how and when this has happened.

Points to ponder in group discussion or private journaling:

1. As you interacted with God, what did you hear from Him?

2. What was the biggest aha moment from this section?

3. Based on what you learned in this session, identify one action you can take that would be helpful.

CHAPTER 6

DEEP RAVINES

Read or reread chapter 6 in *Unstuck*.

Main Ideas

Here is a list of the main ideas you'll find in chapter 6:
- When we grow up in dysfunctional homes, ditchy behaviors can become our "normal."
- Becoming aware of ditchy behaviors can help you change the patterns.
- The dysfunctional generational pattern can stop with you.
- As children, we are limited in ways to cope with trauma.
- Even when we're stuck in deep ravines, there's hope to climb out by using the same principles we employ for climbing out of any ditch.
- When we hurt someone else, we also hurt ourselves and vice versa.
- Whether we experienced abuse or caused it, we will feel shame.
- Deep-Ravine Behaviors are fueled by intense fear, which manifests through various forms of fight, flight, or freeze responses.
- Violence shows up in words and deeds against others and against self.
- Unresolved traumatic experiences keep us locked in unhealthy relationships and behaviors.
- Fight, flight, and freeze are knee-jerk reactions to a current event that is triggered by the intense feeling of powerlessness we experienced as a child.
- Fight manifests as lashing out at others. Flight shows up in some manner of escape, whether physical, mental, or emotional. Freeze results in our inability to take action.

- Identifying shame and letting it go helps us find freedom.
- Recovery groups can help us heal.
- Healing from our bad experiences can help us learn to trust God.
- Growing in awareness and tackling one behavior at a time empowers us to overcome the fears that trap us.

DEEP RAVINES: SESSION 1

In this chapter, we will look at deep ravines into which we may have figuratively been born, pushed, fallen, or jumped into. These ravines are characterized by the ditchy behaviors listed in the appendix of *Unstuck*. When born in a ravine, our caregivers or parents modeled some very unhealthy behaviors.

The goal is to become aware of the types of behaviors you experienced as a child. Some of those things may still be happening today, some you may have forgotten, and some you may have already consciously decided to change. Those things still going on today are part of your "normal" from childhood that stuck with you into adulthood. By doing this work, you finally get to consciously decide if you want to create a new normal!

Review the Ditch Behaviors Checklist I've provided on the next page. The least painful way to do this is to imagine yourself as a stranger observing yourself as a child. Try to disconnect from your feelings and observe the memories that come up for you while you go through this exercise.

If your anxiety rises to a level 4 during the exercise, stop and put those emotions into your container before continuing. Resume when you are ready; remember, you don't have to do this in one sitting. Take your time and go through it at your own pace. If going through this list draws up many painful emotions, you may want to break this exercise into smaller chunks.

Ditchy Behaviors:[1]

Mark an "O" if someone else behaved this way toward you and "Y" if you have acted out this behavior. Some or many of these will have both an O and a Y because the tendency is to repeat what was done to us without realizing it, hurting others and ourselves in the process.

_____ Accusing
_____ Addictions
_____ Affairs
_____ Attacking
_____ Attitude of superiority, dominance, pride ("I'm better than you!")

_____ Bait and switch (promising something, then not following through)
_____ Belittling
_____ Biting
_____ Blaming
_____ Blocking access to others
_____ Blocking exit or entry
_____ Bossing
_____ Brandishing a weapon
_____ Breaking bones
_____ Breaking things
_____ Bruising
_____ Causing job loss
_____ Causing injuries
_____ Causing intentional suffering
_____ Choking
_____ Coercion
_____ Concussions
_____ Controlling access to others
_____ Crazymaking (one minute one way, suddenly the opposite)
_____ Criticizing
_____ Cursing at someone
_____ Demanding something, then punishing for doing it
_____ Demanding to know another's whereabouts at all times
_____ Demeaning
_____ Denying input from others
_____ Denying that an incident happened when it really did
_____ Destroying personal property belonging to another
_____ Dishonesty
_____ Disposing of or destroying someone else's mementos
_____ Double standards: it's okay for one but not okay for the other
_____ Drinking too much
_____ Drugs
_____ Eavesdropping

_____ Embarrassing others
_____ Evasiveness
_____ False accusations
_____ Forced sex
_____ Forced to stay in one position for an unreasonable or extreme length of time
_____ Gambling (addictive)
_____ Getting close to one's face in a menacing way
_____ Getting rid of a child's things without their consent
_____ Grooming (saying nice things, giving gifts with the ultimate goal to control in some way)
_____ Hair pulling
_____ Having to account for all of one's time
_____ Hitting
_____ Humiliation
_____ Hurting or killing pets
_____ Hurting others
_____ Inconsistent: going from one extreme to the other
_____ Intentionally causing pain
_____ Interfering with work
_____ Intimidating
_____ Invalidating someone by interrupting them, saying they shouldn't feel that way, or not allowing another to speak
_____ Isolating a person from others
_____ Kicking
_____ Locking someone in a confined space or room
_____ Lying
_____ Making fun of someone
_____ Manipulating
_____ Menacing looks
_____ Minimizing the seriousness of a situation
_____ Misusing medication
_____ Mocking

- _____ Name-calling (calling someone lazy, good for nothing, stupid, clumsy, etc.)
- _____ Not allowed to go anywhere alone (as an adult)
- _____ Not allowed to have your own opinion
- _____ Not allowed to say what you think or feel
- _____ Not ever allowing others to win
- _____ Opening another's mail
- _____ Passive-aggressive behaviors
- _____ Pinching
- _____ Pornography
- _____ Punching
- _____ Pushing
- _____ Put-downs
- _____ Rape
- _____ Refusing to allow medical care for injuries
- _____ Restricting access to shared money
- _____ Shaming
- _____ Slapping
- _____ Spanking too hard or for too long
- _____ Spitting
- _____ Squandering family money so there isn't enough for basics
- _____ Stalking
- _____ Stealing
- _____ Swearing at someone
- _____ Taking away one's ID cards (green card, passport, driver's license)
- _____ Taking one's money or phone
- _____ Taunting
- _____ Tearing up photos
- _____ Threatening gestures, blackmail, or harm
- _____ Threatening punishment by God, courts, police, juvenile detention, foster homes, or relatives
- _____ Threats to report to authorities (whether parents or officials) that are untrue

_____ Threats to take or kidnap the children
_____ Throwing objects
_____ Throwing objects directed at a person
_____ Tone of voice is harsh and severe
_____ Tying up
_____ Using a welt-producing object to spank
_____ Using children as one's confidant inappropriately
_____ Using others as go-betweens (especially children)
_____ Using weapons (knife, gun, club, stick, etc.)
_____ Violent sex
_____ When one brings up something bothersome, the other turns it back to the other
_____ Withholding basic needs from others (food, clothing, housing, school, etc.)
_____ Withholding child support

Self-harming behaviors:

For the following actions, the O will represent something a little different. Since these are self-harming behaviors, allow the O to mean it was a behavior you witnessed another family member doing. The Y indicates you did this.

_____ Anorexia
_____ Anything to an excessive degree: working, eating, exercising, drinking, drugs, sex, gaming
_____ Attempting suicide
_____ Bulimia
_____ Cutting
_____ Depriving self of basic needs or enjoyment
_____ Lying in bed or on the couch all day
_____ Numbing out through addictive or repetitive activities
_____ Prescription medicine dependence/addiction
_____ Self-injury
_____ Shutting down
_____ Slamming head or body against a wall or other object
_____ Suicidal thoughts

_____ Taking the blame for everything
_____ Threats to commit suicide
_____ Withdrawing
_____ Other: _____

Remember to place anything disturbing or unresolved into your container.

Is there anything you would like to put in your container? If so, do it now. Feel free to make a note of what you put away.

Now go back and count up how many Os and Ys that you have.

Number of Os = _____

Number of Ys = _____

1. What realizations did you gain from this exercise?

2. What is the one behavior you would most like to change? Figure out what you'd like to do instead, then start working on that.

3. What would you like to do instead of that behavior?

4. Rewarding yourself for positive action instead of punishing yourself for forgetting will help you accomplish change more quickly. How will you reward yourself after you've done the new desired behavior instead of the old reaction after five, ten, and twenty times?

5. How will you celebrate when you've successfully eliminated the undesirable behavior?

My prayer over you:
Dear God, I pray for this dear reader as You provide the power to change patterns, habits, and behaviors. Eliminate those behaviors that no longer serve them or those around them. Protect them from feeling overwhelmed over the changes they'd like to make in their lives or the shame they may feel. Remind them that big changes happen in tiny increments. Give them hope and encouragement along the way. In Jesus' name, amen.

Conversation starters with God:
Now it's your turn to pray. Find a quiet place. Bring a journal and pen if you enjoy writing your prayers. Above all, be prepared to listen to what God has to say to you in response. And because prayer is a conversation with someone who knows and loves you, here are a few conversations starters to get the ball rolling:

Dear God,
- What do You most want for me to take away from today's session?
- My family passed on so many unhealthy behaviors, so where do I start to make changes?
- Which behaviors and in what order do You want me to focus on first to work on overcoming?
- How do You want me to celebrate my progress?

Points to ponder in group discussion or private journaling:

1. As you interacted with God, what did you hear from Him?

2. What was the biggest aha moment from this section?

3. Based on what you learned in this session, identify one action you can take that would be helpful.

CHAPTER 7

DITCHING PEOPLE

Read or reread chapter 7 in *Unstuck*.

Main Ideas

Here is a list of the main ideas you'll find in chapter 7:
- Do you need to ditch a person or association with an organization that is tearing you down and keeping you stuck?
- We may have tried *everything we know* to do, but it doesn't mean we've tried *everything*.
- Options exist outside of our sphere of knowledge and awareness.
- Instead of trying to get a spouse to change, focus on what you can change within yourself.
- In some situations, the best move may be a temporary or permanent separation from a toxic relationship.
- Evaluate all the reasons for your decision, then select the best option for everyone involved.
- Get help to guide you through the decision-making process.
- Avoid hanging around people who blatantly reject God or drag you into wrong behavior.
- Don't let others control you. If you feel controlled, get help to set better boundaries.
- You may need to muster all the resources available to you to break the generational legacy of bad relationships.
- Take a close look at the reasons that have been keeping you stuck, then develop a plan to start getting out. Are any of these things keeping you stuck?

- Ingrained fear of failure
- Fear of being blamed for ending the relationship
- Fear of what others will think
- Financial dependence
- Emotional dependence
- Waiting for the other person to change
- Listening to the naysayers in your life
- Afraid to take action for fear of how others will react
- Feeling paralyzed
- Fear of being alone
- Carefully evaluate your part and act on that knowledge.
- Evaluate how ditchy the behaviors are.
- Look at your partner's good qualities.
- Evaluate the reasons you remain stuck.
- If you decide to separate, let go of what you anticipate will happen.
- Plan to reevaluate your decision in three or six months.
- Every relationship comes with baggage. Get help. It's worth it.
- Determining to change for the better in your current relationship is the healthiest thing you can do. It's also the hardest, but it comes with the biggest payoff, especially if you have kids. They learned from your example what an unhealthy relationship looked like. Now they will experience and see the contrast of what it looks like to develop a healthy relationship. They also get to have both parents under one roof.
- Your choices may influence your partner to do their own healing work, but that should not be the motivation for your actions.
- Determine the best move, take everyone involved into consideration (including yourself), do the work, and leave the results to God.

DITCHING PEOPLE: SESSION 1

Are you involved in a group, organization, or community that is dragging you down to the point where trust in your ability to hold your own ground is lost?

If so, the fact that you haven't already done something about your situation proves the difficulty of taking action. The thought of making a change in response to what you learn in this chapter may be absolutely terrifying! And rightly so. So let's break this down into smaller pieces so it becomes a little more manageable.

1. The first step? Identify any groups or community you're involved in—work, family, religious, academic, professional—that you suspect are toxic:

2. What have you tried so far to remedy the situation? Perhaps you have suggested changes within the community or have tried in vain to extricate and protect yourself in the past. List everything you can think of. It's no use trying things that didn't work, so it's important to identify what you've already tried.

3. Is there any person or group with whom you are involved that opposes or rejects God? If so, who?

4. What organizations or communities may be having a negative influence on you? Sometimes people stick around because they believe their good example will influence the others to give up their bad actions. However, most of the time the negative people overshadow the positive people.

5. With whom do you feel controlled?

6. In what ways do you feel controlled?

7. List all the problems in this relationship.

8. What are some of the ways the person/organization reacts that keeps you from doing what you'd like to do or saying what you need to say?

9. What do you believe about your predicament? List everything that comes to mind. (For example: *I'm trapped. I can't leave. It's my fault. I don't have the money or resources. What would people think?*)

Before you decide to ditch a person or an organization, be sure to review the guidelines in chapter 11, the Path to Empowerment. This way you can be sure you have considered all aspects of the issue. Doing so will help ensure you are solid about your decision.

10. How many years has this difficulty been going on?

11. Have you considered going to counseling or receiving life coaching to get some help regarding this problem? Yes _____ No _____

Is there anything you would like to put in your container? If so, do it now. Feel free to make a note of what you put away.

It takes a lot of courage to take a hard look at this situation! Chances are, the problem has been going on for a long time, and the repercussions are significant. However, the rewards for making the right decision will be well worth it. Hats off to you for being willing to examine the issue in greater depth!

My prayer over you:
Dear God, I pray for this dear reader as they begin to face the realities of their situation. Please provide wisdom and guidance in moving forward. Place the right people in their path to help navigate their circumstances in the best way possible. In Jesus' name, amen.

Conversation starters with God:
Now it's your turn to pray. Find a quiet place. Bring a journal and pen if you enjoy writing your prayers. Above all, be prepared to listen to what God has to say to you in response. And because prayer is a conversation with someone who knows and loves you, here are a few conversations starters to get the ball rolling:

Dear God,
- What do You most want for me to take away from today's session?
- Facing this situation is so scary! Where do I begin? Help me to identify all the what-ifs, and show me how to address them.
- What are the potential benefits of me changing how I've responded in this situation? Show me how to have hope.

Points to ponder in group discussion or private journaling:
1. As you interacted with God, what did you hear from Him?

2. What was the biggest aha moment from this section?

3. Based on what you learned in this session, identify one action you can take that would be helpful.

DITCHING PEOPLE: SESSION 2

This session directs our attention to one-on-one relationships, primarily significant others. However, the same principles apply to any relationship you have. Perhaps your issue is with a friend or relative, not your partner, so make adaptations as needed. The questions are intended to bring to light considerations that will help lead to the best option for your situation.

1. Have you asked your spouse to go to counseling? Yes _____ No _____
   If your partner said no, you may feel stuck and believe going by yourself won't help.
   However, a good therapist can assist you in identifying what you can do differently, which will help you get unstuck. You'll benefit from an outside perspective, which you'll need whether you continue the relationship or decide to leave. When you do something different, your partner's attempts to push you into your ditch or cause you to run to your ditch won't be as effective.

2. What are your fears about going to counseling on your own?

3. Proverbs 11:14 tells us, "Where there is no counsel, the people fall; But in the multitude of counselors there is safety." The bigger the decision, the more input we need to help us make the wisest choice. Who are your advisors?

4. If you sought help, what was your experience?

   If previous counseling didn't seem helpful, perhaps the therapist was not a good fit for you or didn't have the expertise necessary to help you. Consider trying someone else, and keep searching until you find a professional who is a good fit and can help you. There are a lot of good therapists out there.

5. If a temporary separation were an option, where would you consider going to live or asking your partner to go? Are separate bedrooms a possibility?

6. What are the things you strongly dislike about your partner?

7. What are some ways you can begin to respond differently to the irritating things your partner says or does? Considering in advance what you will say or do does wonders to help you change how you react when triggered by another. However, big change happens in small increments, so be patient with yourself and others with the transformation process.

8. Who else do you need to consider in your decision to end the relationship? It's important to remember to value what you want equally with the desires and needs of others. Getting outside guidance and input can help you ensure you are making the best decision for all involved, including yourself.

9. List the worst ditchy behaviors that have taken place in the relationship. (Often, we feel so much shame from this happening to us or acting in ditchy ways ourselves that we want to block those things out. But if they remain blocked, there is a greater chance of repetition.) Bringing these into the light is the first step toward a better tomorrow. If you're not ready to share with another what has happened to you, at least acknowledge the truth to yourself and to God. You can be real with God. He already knows, so it's mainly about becoming honest with yourself.

10. What are the positive characteristics and strengths of your relationship? Whether it's due to a long history, shared memories, common faith, or raising children, there are a number of compelling reasons that have kept you in this relationship. It's important to look at both the good and bad of the relationship as you make the wisest decision possible for your future. It may

seem your spouse will never change, but that doesn't keep you from deciding to make your life better.

11. In what ways would you and your family benefit if you ditched the unhealthy behaviors instead of the relationship? (Remember, if you leave, unless you make big changes, you carry the way you relate into your future relationships.)

12. As you seek God's input in your situation, what do you sense He is guiding you to do?

13. What scriptures support the sense you have?

14. What are your reasons for staying stuck? Common reasons: "If I leave, that means I'm a failure." "I fear being blamed for ending the relationship." "I fear what others will think." "I am financially and emotionally dependent, waiting for the other person to change." "I'm listening to the people who tell me I can't." I'm afraid to take action for fear of how others will react." "I feel paralyzed." List all the reasons that come to mind.

15. What do you stand to gain by doing the hard work of climbing out of your ditch and changing how you relate to those around you?

16. What's your plan for crawling out of your ditch? List three steps you will take. One of those could be completing this study guide.

> **Is there anything you would like to put in your container? If so, do it now. Feel free to make a note of what you put away.**

Taking a hard look at whether to ditch an organization, community, or relationship brings up lots of mixed, scary feelings. However, there is freedom in having the courage to look objectively at the situation. When we begin to move away from the ditch in which we're lodged, we can enter onto the road of a healthier, happier life.

My prayer over you:
Dear God, I pray for this dear reader as they figure out the best course of action. Please give wisdom, guidance, and courage to face what must be faced. Help them to overcome the fear of change, fear of the unknown, fear of making life worse, fear of being alone, fear of speaking up, fear of what others will think, fear of making the wrong decision, and all the other fears that show up as the reader works through this. In Jesus' name, amen.

Conversation starters with God:
Now it's your turn to pray. Find a quiet place. Bring a journal and pen if you enjoy writing your prayers. Above all, be prepared to listen to what God has to say to you in response. And because prayer is a conversation with someone who knows and loves you, here are a few conversations starters to get the ball rolling:

Dear God,
- What do You most want for me to take away from today's session?
- What organization or relationship do You want me to closely examine?
- Who can I turn to for help? I don't know of anyone I can trust.

Points to ponder in group discussion or private journaling:
1. As you interacted with God, what did you hear from Him?

2. What was the biggest aha moment from this section?

3. Based on what you learned in this session, identify one action you can take that would be helpful.

CHAPTER 8

BUILDING A PATH OUT OF THE DITCH

Read or reread chapter 8 in *Unstuck*.

Main Ideas

Here is a list of the main ideas you'll find in chapter 8:
- To come out of the Others-Focused Ditch, you must take your own thoughts, feelings, concerns, and desires into account.
- Sometimes forward progress looks more like sideways bleachers.
- Our brain must tear down our old way of doing things, then integrate into a new construct what gets deleted, added, modified, or stays the same.
- Big change happens in tiny increments, like the time it takes for a cruise ship to leave port.
- Seek God in prayer, and ask for help from those you trust.
- Break down the change process into small, manageable chunks.
- Get in touch with your feelings.
- Look for the small actions you took instead of all the times you reverted to your old behaviors.
- Focus on changing one thing at a time.

A PATH OUT OF THE DITCH: SESSION 1

We're now getting to the good stuff! The first seven chapters have provided a close look at life in the ditch. You've grown by leaps and bounds in the awareness of your ditchy behaviors—your behavior and the behavior of others. That is h-u-g-e!

Now we are going to begin constructing our path out. Our first step involves noticing which default got triggered. So let's start there.

1. When do you tend to operate from the Others-Focused Ditch, solely considering another person's thoughts, feelings, concerns, and desires and not your own?

2. Are there certain topics of conversation that seem to trigger this behavior? Or certain circumstances in which it occurs?

3. During what types of conversational topics, or in what situations, do you most forget about others and make decisions for yourself?

4. In what situations have you made balanced decisions that seek the best interests for everyone involved?

It's as important to notice what you're doing right as it is to identify what needs improvement. Awareness of our healthy actions breeds more of the same.

5. Prior to reading chapter 8 of *Unstuck*, what did your change process graph look like? (Draw it in the box below.)

6. In what ways does it help to know the mental processes our brains engage in order to process change? How does the visual of "sideways bleachers" help you?

7. What struck you about the illustration of change being like a cruise ship leaving port and heading toward the open sea?

8. At one point in my life, whenever I missed the mark while working on changing, my internal dialogue would be critical and judgmental: *There, you screwed up again. Can't you ever get it right? You're never going to get this down.* A conscious decision to think and say accurate, positive things helps with the process of changing. What new affirmations will you tell yourself and others during your process of change? Highlight the ones that you think will be most useful to you:
    - "I forgot to implement change today, but I will keep working at it."
    - "I thought about the new way once this week. That's more than I thought about it last week!"
    - "My spouse forgot, but I can see the efforts being made. Change is a process."
    - "I'm relieved to know I don't have to be perfect at these changes right away. I will give myself (and others) grace when either of us forget or revert to our old ways. Then I will talk about or consider what I want things to look like going forward."
    - "I refuse to judge or criticize myself (or others) for my tendency to fall, run to, or feel pushed into ditches. This is going to take time, and I'm in it for the long haul."
    - "Eventually, I'll consistently be on the road."

9. Add your own affirmations that you plan to tell yourself during the time period in which you are learning new ways of responding:

10. What Ditch Behavior are you working on changing?

11. To help yourself with the change process, create a reward plan. You might keep a record of your change efforts on a chart on the refrigerator, at your desk, or on your cell phone. Mark every time you did what you wanted to do. Do not focus on the mistakes or forgotten times. Keep your focus on what you are doing right. Reward yourself incrementally. At first, you might celebrate after five times you remembered the new response, then ten, then fifteen, then stretch it out to twenty-five and so on. Plan ahead how you will treat yourself for your accomplishments at each juncture, then consider planning a bigger celebration once the new behavior has been well established. What reward system will you create for yourself to celebrate your progress?

**Is there anything you would like to put in your container? If so, do it now.
Feel free to make a note of what you put away.**

It's exciting to know we're finally getting traction on shifting reactions to responses! With persistence, those ditchy behaviors will be left in the dust, and you'll be experiencing a much smoother ride on the road. Remember, you've already made some adjustments in thinking, and that is change!

My prayer over you:

Dear God, I pray for this dear reader, and I thank You for helping them understand the process of change at a deeper level. Help them see they don't have to be perfect in the process. Please help this reader change through Christ who gives them strength. In Jesus' name, amen.

Conversation starters with God:

Now it's your turn to pray. Find a quiet place. Bring a journal and pen if you enjoy writing your prayers. Above all, be prepared to listen to what God has to say to you in response. And because prayer is a conversation with someone who knows and loves you, here are a few conversations starters to get the ball rolling:

Dear God,
- What do You most want for me to take away from today's session?
- What truth do You want me to use to replace the lie I've been believing that has kept me stuck?
- Show me where I've expected change to happen immediately and been disappointed when it hasn't. In what ways can I show patience with myself as I'm working on changing?

Points to ponder in group discussion or private journaling:
1. As you interacted with God, what did you hear from Him?

2. What was the biggest aha moment from this section?

3. Based on what you learned in this session, identify one action you can take that would be helpful.

CHAPTER 9

STEPPING-STONES FOR CRAWLING OUT OF THE DITCH

Read or reread chapter 9 in *Unstuck*.

Main Ideas

Here is a list of the main ideas you'll find in chapter 9:
- Begin to notice:
  - the topic
  - your ditch
  - your default behaviors
  - your partner's ditch and their behavior
  - the fears driving your and your partner's action
- Change how you start conversations:[1]
  - Notice and adjust your tone of voice.
  - Shift how you form questions and statements.

STEPPING-STONES FOR CRAWLING OUT OF THE DITCH: SESSION 1

We're actually making some real headway on living our best life. Thanks for hanging in there! This chapter focuses on "noticing" and "modifying communication."[2] Therefore, we're going to go step by step to increase your chances of success.

As stated in the book *Unstuck,* noticing consists of five elements.

Think back to the last argument you had with someone, and answer the following questions relative to that event.

1. Take note of the topic when the Ditch Behaviors emerged. The topic was:

2. Identify the ditch.
   a. Is it Others-Focused, Me-Focused, or both?

   b. What did your partner say or do that triggered you, or what did you say or do that set the other person off?

3. What were your default behaviors?

What did you want or need that you couldn't voice at the time?

4. Identify your partner's ditch.
   a. Is it Others-Focused, Me-Focused, or both?

   b. What did you say or do that triggered your partner, or what did he/she say or do that set you off?

5. Name the fears related to the situation or topic.

Now we shift to examining how we tend to start up a conversation.[3] Often, it's so ingrained and automatic that we don't know exactly how we say what we say. Therefore, I'll start by having you write down what you would say in the following situations so you'll know what needs tweaking and what's working well.
1. How do you ask someone to go to a restaurant or activity with you? Write down how you would phrase your question:

2. How do you start the conversation when you're upset with certain people? For example, how do you respond when the kitchen was left a mess or when something was supposed to be done didn't happen. Write down what you would say to each of the following:

   a. To your mate:

   b. To your children:

   c. To a guest:

3. When a family member returns home and you'd like that person to do something, how do you greet him or her?

   Read your answers to someone else and ask: a) if the wording of the question was clear, b) if it caused a feeling of defensiveness, and c) if different wording would feel better. Ideally, share this with the people you live with to get their input and feedback.

4. Of the start-up questions you wrote above, which did not include an "I want" or "I would like"? Which had the word "you" in it but no "I"?

5. Have a discussion with family members about the tone—yours and theirs—when upset. Don't have the discussion when you're upset; have the discussion when you're both in a good place, then talk about the tone that comes up when emotions run high. Discuss how you can navigate the next conflict in a better way.

6. How do you express to your children that something must be completed before they can have free time?

7. If your statement includes a negative, how could you say it in a way that offers a reward instead of a consequence?

8. What are some of the messages of obligation you received during childhood, such as "You should . . ." "You ought to . . ." "You can't unless . . ." "You have to . . ." or "You need to . . ."?

9. List some common phrases you or your family use that involve a negative approach to a conversation or situation. Examples: "Why don't we go for a hike?" or "You can't go until your work is done."

10. What are some of the ways you feel attacked, overpowered, or shut down by others?

11. Who in your family tends to approach things more directly, and who tends to be more passive in their approach?

> **Is there anything you would like to put in your container? If so, do it now. Feel free to make a note of what you put away.**

The suggestions in this chapter form the tip of the iceberg of improving communication skills. I highly recommend checking out www.CoupleTalk.com.[4] There you can learn ten skills that will improve your effectiveness in working through conflict, expressing your thoughts and feelings, increasing ability to empathize with what others say, and feeling heard. If some people say to you, "I don't feel heard," when it's you who doesn't feel heard, or if you have recurring arguments that don't get resolved, CoupleTalk is for you. Even though CoupleTalk is geared for couples, you can still learn the skills with a friend, relative, or group of friends. You'll be blessed for the rest of your life if you do.

My prayer over you:
Dear God, I pray for this dear reader as they begin to work on improving communication skills. Please give them patience as they work through changes, develop persistence to keep at it, and sharpen their ability to celebrate the progress they make. In Jesus' name, amen.

Conversation starters with God:
Now it's your turn to pray. Find a quiet place. Bring a journal and pen if you enjoy writing your prayers. Above all, be prepared to listen to what God has to say to you in response. And because prayer is a conversation with someone who knows and loves you, here are a few conversations starters to get the ball rolling:

Dear God,
- What do You most want for me to take away from today's session?
- My patterns of communication are so deeply ingrained! Show me examples of when I reverted to my old way of saying things.
- What phrase or sentence do I need to start working on changing first?

Points to ponder in group discussion or private journaling:

1. As you interacted with God, what did you hear from Him?

2. What was the biggest aha moment from this section?

3. Based on what you learned in this session, identify one action you can take that would be helpful.

CHAPTER 10

THE ABCDS OF NEGATIVE INTERACTIONS

Read or reread chapter 10 in *Unstuck*.

Main Ideas

Here's a list of the main ideas you'll find in chapter 10:
- The ABCDs of negative interactions represent: <u>A</u>ttacking, <u>B</u>laming, <u>C</u>riticizing, and <u>D</u>efending.[1]
- <u>A</u>ttack:
    - Tell, suggest, or hint at what someone should do.
    - Engage in name-calling or labeling someone's behavior.
    - Tell someone what they did to you.
    - Sarcastic, irate, irritated, angry, annoyed, mocking, or demeaning tone or attitude.
- <u>B</u>lame:
    - Assign all the blame to the other person.
- <u>C</u>riticize:
    - Point out the faults, flaws, and failures of others.
- <u>D</u>efending or <u>D</u>eflecting :
    - Refuse to share any responsibility.
    - Deflect attacks, accusations, blame, or criticism by attacking, accusing, criticizing, or blaming right back.

THE ABCDS OF NEGATIVE INTERACTIONS: SESSION 1

We're over half finished with this study guide. What an accomplishment! If you have been diligent to complete the questions, you now have more awareness than I had for over fifty years! That means you are positioned to have a much happier, more successful life where you're on the road more often than in the ditch. Each successful interaction with others causes you to feel better; conversely, each conversation that left you feeling powerless added to your misery.

This chapter is divided into two sessions. The first session is devoted to identifying how and what you currently say in a variety of situations when feeling attacked, criticized, or blamed. The second session will guide you into finding more effective ways of expressing yourself.

I was unaware when I attacked others. You may be too. It will be valuable to spend a little time considering when you or other people in your household speak in ways that are a veiled—or not so veiled—attack. We learned from our parents' speech patterns and conversation start-up approaches, so what I am describing may seem "normal" to you. However, because you're invested in creating a happier way of living, it's beneficial to see where these patterns crop up.

1. Identify up to five examples of the following kinds of communication (or commonplace circumstances in which you often respond this way): telling, suggesting, or hinting at what someone else should do. Examples: "You need to get that bill in the mail tomorrow." "It would be nice if someone made me some tea."

    a. _____
    b. _____
    c. _____
    d. _____
    e. _____

THE ABCDS OF NEGATIVE INTERACTIONS 167

2. Identify up to five examples of the following kinds of communication (or commonplace circumstances in which you often respond this way). For example, name calling or labeling of someone's behavior: "You slacker!" or "You're irritating me!"
   a. _____
   b. _____
   c. _____
   d. _____
   e. _____

3. Identify up to five examples of the following kinds of communication (or commonplace circumstances in which you often respond this way): telling someone what they did to you. Examples: "You hurt my feelings." "You never listen!" Include "always" and "never" statements, such as, "You're always late."
   a. _____
   b. _____
   c. _____
   d. _____
   e. _____

4. Identify up to five examples of the following kinds of communication (or commonplace circumstances in which you often respond this way): Your attitude is irate, irritated, angry, annoyed, mocking, or demeaning. Example: "You make me mad!"
   a. _____
   b. _____
   c. _____
   d. _____
   e. _____

5. Identify up to five examples of the following kinds of communication (or commonplace circumstances in which you often respond this way): You tell

someone it's their fault or blame them for something. Examples: "You didn't pick up your room." Or "It's your fault we're late."

a. _____
b. _____
c. _____
d. _____
e. _____

6. Identify up to five examples of the following kinds of communication (or commonplace circumstances in which you often respond this way): You point out the faults, flaws, or failures of others. Examples: "Your shirt is wrinkled." Or "Why can't you get that through your thick head?"

a. _____
b. _____
c. _____
d. _____
e. _____

7. Identify up to five examples of the following kinds of communication (or commonplace circumstances in which you often respond this way): Did you defend yourself and not take any responsibility when attacked, accused, or blamed for something? Examples: "It's not my fault the trash didn't get put out." Or "You didn't do what you were supposed to do either!"

a. _____
b. _____
c. _____
d. _____
e. _____

8. Identify up to five examples of the following kinds of communication (or commonplace circumstances in which you often respond this way): You attack, blame, or criticize someone, or you feel attacked, blamed, or criticized.

Example: "I felt attacked when my spouse said, "Where did you put my keys?" Or "How come you're late?"

a. _____
b. _____
c. _____
d. _____
e. _____

To get a sense of the pervasiveness of attacking, blaming, and criticizing, watch a TV soap opera and note when the actors engage in this manner. See the effect it has. Did the people get what they wanted?

Telling someone else what to do isn't always bad. When we're in a learning mode or teaching someone how to do something, it's necessary.

9. Give up to five examples of when it's appropriate to tell someone else what to do. Example: "Don't run into the street!"

a. _____
b. _____
c. _____
d. _____
e. _____

Now you have examples of how you were programmed to say things. In our next session, we will use that information for your learning.

> **Is there anything you would like to put in your container? If so, do it now.**
> **Feel free to make a note of what you put away.**

My prayer over you:

Dear God, I pray for this dear reader as they develop deeper awareness of their communication patterns. Thank You for showing them! In Jesus' name, amen.

Conversation starters with God:

Now it's your turn to pray. Find a quiet place. Bring a journal and pen if you enjoy writing your prayers. Above all, be prepared to listen to what God has to say to you in response. And because prayer is a conversation with someone who knows and loves you, here are a few conversations starters to get the ball rolling:

Dear God,
- What do You most want for me to take away from today's session?
- Are there any other examples You would like to bring to my attention? If yes, what are they?
- Reveal to me ways I'm still judging myself harshly. How do You see me?
- Which of the above do You want me to focus on first?

Points to ponder in group discussion or private journaling:
1. As you interacted with God, what did you hear from Him?

2. What was the biggest aha moment from this section?

3. Based on what you learned in this session, identify one action you can take that would be helpful.

THE ABCDS OF NEGATIVE INTERACTIONS: SESSION 2

Today, we will use your answers from session 1 of chapter 10 to help figure out a better way to express yourself. Look back at what you wrote last session and consider how you would state it from the perspective of how you *felt* about what happened. Change the approach from "you" to "I would like, prefer, need, or want . . ." Or "If you prefer, are willing, or won't mind, please . . ." We have the greatest success at changing when we can take time to think of what we'd like to say in advance. It's much easier than trying to come up with a new way to express yourself on the spot.

1. Reword your examples from question 1: telling, suggesting, or hinting at what someone else should do. Example: "I would like your room to be cleaned by 5:00 p.m. today."

    a. _____
    b. _____
    c. _____
    d. _____
    e. _____

2. Reword the examples of name-calling or labeling of someone's behavior that you've done or heard someone do recently. Examples: "It feels like I'm doing more than you." Or "I feel irritated."

    a. _____
    b. _____
    c. _____
    d. _____
    e. _____

3. Reword the examples of when you told someone what they did to you. Examples: "That hurt my feelings." "I feel unheard!" "I feel worried when you're late."

    a. _____
    b. _____

c. _____
d. _____
e. _____

4. How would you express in a new way the instances in which your attitude was irate, irritated, angry, annoyed, mocking, or demeaning? Example: "I'm feeling annoyed that this is still going on."

   a. _____
   b. _____
   c. _____
   d. _____
   e. _____

5. Write down the new ways you could speak to someone instead of telling them it was their fault or blaming them. Examples: "I'd like you to wear a shirt that's ironed." "I'm frustrated that I can't explain it in a way that you understand."

   a. _____
   b. _____
   c. _____
   d. _____
   e. _____

6. Provide examples of when you have been guilty of doing the same things for which you have criticized another:

   a. _____
   b. _____
   c. _____
   d. _____
   e. _____

7. How will you rewrite your responses when you feel attacked, accused, blamed, or defensive? Example: "I feel put down when you say, 'What were you thinking?'"

   a. _____
   b. _____

c. _____
d. _____
e. _____

> **Is there anything you would like to put in your container? If so, do it now. Feel free to make a note of what you put away.**

This chapter may have been difficult to come up with alternative ways to express yourself. That indicates how automatic our patterns of speaking are! However, your efforts will pay off handsomely as you practice incorporating these new ways of speaking into your daily life. If you struggled to know how to rephrase those statements, discuss them with family members, and brainstorm what wording sounds most acceptable.

My prayer over you:

Dear God, I pray for this dear reader to be patient with the change process and aware when they experience success in rephrasing how they express themselves. Help them persevere through the rest of the chapters because each of these steps helps them walk out of the ditch of powerlessness and fear and onto the road where there is balance, freedom, and a much happier way of life. Thank You for being their support! In Jesus' name, amen.

Conversation starters with God:

Now it's your turn to pray. Find a quiet place. Bring a journal and pen if you enjoy writing your prayers. Above all, be prepared to listen to what God has to say

to you in response. And because prayer is a conversation with someone who knows and loves you, here are a few conversations starters to get the ball rolling:

Dear God,
- What would You have me take away from today's session?
- Bring to my mind phrases that I commonly use that feel attacking, criticizing, or blaming to others, and show me the most effective way of expressing myself.
- Where do You want me to start in applying these new ways of expressing myself?

Points to ponder in group discussion or private journaling:

1. As you interacted with God, what did you hear from Him?

2. What was the biggest aha moment from this section?

3. Based on what you learned in this session, identify one action you can take that would be helpful.

CHAPTER 11

PATH TO EMPOWERMENT: HOW TO STOP ATTACKING AND ACCUSING

Read or reread chapter 11 in *Unstuck*.

Main Ideas

Here is a list of the main ideas you'll find in chapter 11:

Empowerment instead of Attack/Accuse:

Step 1: Identify all the ways you feel:
A. Identify motivations, both personal and altruistic (desire to benefit others).
B. List all the positive thoughts and feelings about the situation.
C. Note all your negative thoughts and feelings about the circumstance.
D. Name the underlying fears you have.

Step 2: Identify how the other person feels:
A. Motivations
B. Positive feelings
C. Negative feelings
D. Fears

Step 3: Look at both sides, and then decide what to do.

Step 4: Take action:
A. Ask or state your request in a different way.
    - Change the way the request is phrased.
    - State clearly what you want.
B. Respond instead of react.
C. Seek wisdom and guidance from God and others.

Step 5: Let go of the outcome. Translation: take action no matter what you think the result will be.

PATH TO EMPOWERMENT: SESSION 1

In this chapter we will examine how to replace our old, powerless methods of expressing our wants and needs—often by attacking and accusing—with a healthier approach. We are going to learn how to identify what we can do or change, then take action on that.

Remember, engaging in our old habits requires *no effort*. They are preprogrammed, automatic reactions. It's normal in our world to blame, criticize, defend, and deflect. But I don't want that kind of "normal" in my life anymore! Do you?

Following, you will find a five-step process to gather information to determine the best option of dealing with a situation.

Select a problem in which you're currently struggling where you want someone else to do something and they are not doing it. Then answer the questions below related to that issue.

Step 1: Identify all the ways you feel about the other person's actions or inaction. I have further broken this down into four parts.

A. What are your motivations for why you want what you want?

1. For your own benefit:

2. For the benefit of others:

B. What are your positive thoughts and feelings about the situation?

C. What are your negative thoughts and feelings related to this topic?

D. Name all of the fears you have about what might or might not happen.

Step 2: Identify how the other person feels or may feel. (If you're on good terms with the individual, you can ask them these questions directly. Often, that's not the case, so do your best to guess what these responses would be.)

A. What do you think the motivations of the person with whom you have conflict are?

1. For their own benefit:

2. For the benefit of others:

B. What do you suppose the other person's positive thoughts and feelings are about the topic?

C. What do you believe the negative thoughts and feelings related to this topic might be?

D. Name all of the fears the other person may have about what might or might not happen.

Step 3: Look at both sides, and then decide what to do. Review the information you wrote down for both you and the person with whom you have been feeling powerless. Brainstorm potential options for addressing the situation. Write all your ideas in your notebook or journal. If you'd like some ideas, check out chapter 16, "What to Do About Fear." So often we are kept paralyzed because of fear. Therefore, many of the strategies used to address fear also help us figure out how to move from powerlessness in a situation to empowerment.

Step 4: Take action! Implement what you decided to do in step 3. Perhaps it requires you to state what you want in a different way.
A. Change the way the request is phrased.[1] For example, If the prior statement was, "You can't go out to play until your room is cleaned." Change it to, "As soon as your room is cleaned, you may go out to play." It may not seem like that's going to do much. However, now they have a reward to look forward to instead of a punishment. When stated the second way, you're empowering your child to be in control of how soon they can start to play. This works equally well with adults. Write down up to five statements, changing the wording from a *consequence* to a *reward*. If you need some ideas, check out LoveandLogic.com for articles, advice, and webinars.[2]

B. State clearly what you want.[3] That means the statement begins with "I want . . ." or "I would like . . ." or "I prefer . . ." instead of saying, "Let's do . . ." or "Why don't we . . . ?" or "Do you want to . . . ?" or "How about us doing . . . ?" If the person says no to a request stated in the latter examples, in essence they are saying no for both of you. Again, this is a subtle but empowering shift. So if I say, "I'd like to go out to dinner tonight. Would you like to go with me?" He or she has the option to say yes, or "No, I'm not up for that tonight." Now you have the option to go by yourself or invite someone else. Think about approaches you regularly used where what you wanted was not clearly stated. Maybe you *thought* they were clearly stated but upon further examination may have been confusing to someone else. Write down how you would say it instead using an "I" statement:

C. After we have made our requests clear, our next step is to figure out what we will do if the person decides not to do what we want them to do. This is the hard part. Be sure you choose an action that is moderate, not extreme. If your child hasn't cleaned his/her room by the stated deadline, then you know when to impose the consequence.
What are some options you might choose?

1. It's most effective to start small and ratchet up, which means set time limits and increase gradually with each infraction.[4] The first time maybe put clothes/toys left out in storage for a day. Next time, it's for two days. The third time, it's for three days. Time for children seems much longer than for adults. (Remember when summers seemed to go on forever?) Shorter times are more effective. You could also have your kids do an extra task to earn their possessions back earlier than the stated time for return. That is empowering and gives them a sense of hope.

2. After considering the age of the person involved, what time length will you use for the first, second, third, and fourth infraction for each person you have in mind?

3. Another strategy involves offering two or three options. Be sure you're happy with all your suggestions. My parents didn't offer options. I went to the opposite extreme and offered too many options. Neither ditch was good. Name up to three situations in which offering two or three options would be helpful.

Step 5: Let go of the outcome. Even if you don't think the person will react in the way you'd like, take action anyway. I used to be able to predict, with just enough accuracy, how I *thought* the other person would respond. That prevented me from taking action because I didn't think it would work. Now, whether what I propose works or not, I'm at least doing something! I've been pleasantly surprised that my new approaches are more effective than I often predicted they would be. I also must be sure I have no expectations attached. If I have hidden expectations, I'm being manipulative.

Remember, changing how you approach situations will take time and practice. At first it's difficult because every part needs to be thought out and compared to our old ways, which are automatic and require no preparation. However, you and your family will love how much more empowered you feel and effective you become as you practice these new ways.

> **Is there anything you would like to put in your container? If so, do it now. Feel free to make a note of what you put away.**

My prayer over you:
Dear God, I pray for this dear reader as they work on incorporating these new ways of responding in situations that have traditionally left them feeling powerless. Give them plenty of grace because they will fall into old patterns more often than they remember the new ones at first. Help them gain traction on this new approach. Thank You for revealing better ways of dealing with situations! In Jesus' name, amen.

Conversation starters with God:
Now it's your turn to pray. Find a quiet place. Bring a journal and pen if you enjoy writing your prayers. Above all, be prepared to listen to what God has to say to you in response. And because prayer is a conversation with someone who knows and loves you, here are a few conversations starters to get the ball rolling:

Dear God,
- What do You most want for me to take away from today's session?
- Reveal ways in which I anticipate my actions will not have the desired effects I want.
- Show me where I have taken action and it worked well.
- Where have I been stymied because I felt powerlessness? Please show me what to do in those situations.

Points to ponder in group discussion or private journaling:
1. As you interacted with God, what did you hear from Him?

2. What was the biggest aha moment from this section?

3. Based on what you learned in this session, identify one action you can take that would be helpful.

CHAPTER 12

PATH TO EMPOWERMENT: HOW TO STOP BLAMING, CRITICIZING, DEFENDING, AND DEFLECTING

Read or reread chapter 12 in *Unstuck*.

Main Ideas

Here is a list of the main ideas you'll find in chapter 12:

Blame
1. Identify your part.
2. Apologize *and* forgive yourself for what you did.
3. Forgive the other person for their portion.
4. Brainstorm for a solution.

Criticism
1. Focus on the good, positive, and praiseworthy.
2. Give genuine compliments.
3. Cultivate gratitude.

Defending / Deflecting
Apply the same principles as those for attacking, criticizing, and blaming.

HOW TO STOP BLAMING, CRITICIZING, DEFENDING, AND DEFLECTING: SESSION 1

In this chapter we continue the process of learning how to replace our old, powerless methods of expressing our wants and needs with healthy approaches. Specifically, we will focus on learning how to shift from blaming, criticizing, defending, and deflecting to a more empowered way of living.

As I mentioned in the book *Unstuck*, blaming, criticizing, defending, and deflecting was alive and well at our house. I used to be quick to blame others but didn't consider how much I hated it when I got blamed for something, even if it was my fault! I especially abhorred it when I was innocent and still got blamed. If I hated it so much, I figured others must hate it too! Therefore, I was determined to find a new way to do life.

Blame

Following is a four-step process for dealing with those times when you'd love to blame someone. You know by now that blaming just keeps you frustrated, angry, and powerless, even when that person is at fault. Here's what you can do instead to keep yourself empowered. Consider a situation when you blamed someone in the past, then go through the following questions in response to that scenario.

1. **What was your part in the problem?**
   Sometimes we can readily identify our part. Other times our role may be passive. Or maybe it's something you were supposed to do but didn't. Occasionally, it's being at the wrong place at the wrong time. Write down your role, no matter how small it seemed to be.

2. **Apologize and forgive yourself for your words or actions.**
   Sometimes an apology to the other party is necessary; sometimes it's not feasible. To the extent possible, extend an apology. It's critically important to forgive

yourself; otherwise anger at yourself compounds the anger projected onto others—often not even the person at whom you feel angry!

Write out an apology and statement of forgiveness below.

3. **Forgive the other person for their role.**

    Yes, that's a tall order, but it's for *your* sake. It will be a process, yet that's how we are set free from bitterness. For what do you need to forgive someone?

4. **Brainstorm for a solution.**

    Finding a way to solve the problem or resolve the issue is what moves us forward.

    Come up with a plan or jot down some thoughts about how to resolve the issue.

Criticism

I don't think anyone would raise their hand and say, "I like getting criticized." Yet we all have been guilty of criticizing others, especially family members. Jesus said, "Do to others as you would have them do to you" (Luke 6:31 NIV).

The following three practices may be helpful:
1. Focus on the good, positive, and praiseworthy.
    Provide up to five examples of actions that were good, positive, and praiseworthy in the last month.

2. Cultivate a habit of complimenting others.
    List up to five times you have complimented someone in the last month with no expectations of anything in return.

3. Be mindful of gratitude.
    Note up to five instances you have been grateful or shown gratitude in the last month.

4. If in 1, 2, or 3 above you did not list up to five things, identify some options for increasing your focus on what is good, positive, and praiseworthy. Increase the frequency of intentional compliments, or increase thankfulness and gratitude.

Defend / Deflect

We employ the same strategies to counter defending and deflecting that we already explained in the sections on attacking/accusing, blaming, and criticizing. Furthermore, the following suggestions could also be helpful. You can say, "I'm feeling attacked. Will you please rephrase what you said?" Or "Instead of labeling what I'm doing, please explain to me how you feel about what I did." Note: it is easy to identify when someone else gets defensive, but it may be difficult to understand what you said or did that caused their defensive reaction to you.

1. Think of a situation in which you felt defensive. How will you handle a similar situation differently if it comes up in the future?

2. You are well on your way down the path to empowerment! Few people have come as far as you have. It's time to celebrate. Write down some options for celebrating your progress. It doesn't have to be costly or require much planning.

> **Is there anything you would like to put in your container? If so, do it now. Feel free to make a note of what you put away.**

My prayer over you:

Dear God, I pray for this dear reader as You show them healthier ways to live and interact with others. Thank You for revealing this! Help each reader to quickly adopt these new practices. In Jesus' name, amen.

Conversation starters with God:

Now it's your turn to pray. Find a quiet place. Bring a journal and pen if you enjoy writing your prayers. Above all, be prepared to listen to what God has to say to you in response. And because prayer is a conversation with someone who knows and loves you, here are a few conversations starters to get the ball rolling:

Dear God,
- What do You most want for me to take away from today's session?
- When have I blamed others and refused to take any ownership of the situation? Reveal it to me so I can live in a more empowered way.
- Reveal to me positive things in the people I see only negatively.
- Show me things I can be grateful for in my life, and give me the courage to express that gratitude to others.

Points to ponder in group discussion or private journaling:

1. As you interacted with God, what did you hear from Him?

2. What was the biggest aha moment from this section?

3. Based on what you learned in this session, identify one action you can take that would be helpful.

CHAPTER 13

FROM THE OTHERS-FOCUSED DITCH TO THE ROAD

Read or reread chapter 13 in *Unstuck*.

Main Ideas

Here is a list of the main ideas you'll find in chapter 13:

Following, in a nutshell, are suggestions for overcoming Others-Focused Ditch Behaviors:

1. People-pleasing: Change your internal dialogue to value yourself equally with others.
2. Default answer *yes*: Give yourself time to think before answering, and allow yourself to change your yes to no.
3. Readily giving up what you want: Think through and decide what you want.
4. Difficulty making decisions: Choose to accept responsibility for your decisions and decide to let go of what other people might think about what you do.
5. Walking on eggshells: Brainstorm for options, name your fears, and decide to let go of how you think others will react.
6. Difficulty expressing feelings or opinions: Identify and name what you feel, practice stating how you feel with safe people, and decide to value your feelings even when others disagree.
7. Avoiding: Learn to express yourself more effectively by learning Relationship Enhancement® skills available at nire.org or CoupleTalk.com.

8. Codependence: Recognize you have security that God will never reject you; therefore, you can face the potential rejection of others, even if it is painful. Learn to discern what you can actually control and what you have no control over.
9. Blaming: Swallow any self-righteous pride and identify and acknowledge your part in a situation even if it is very small, apologize for it, forgive yourself and others for their part, and brainstorm to find a solution.
10. Being passive: Figure out what you want, then pursue that goal.
11. Feeling obligated: Figure out if you truly are the only one who can accomplish the task, and then decide if it fits in your list of priorities.
12. Being resentful: Decide not to do something if you will resent doing it. Forgive others for past resentments.
13. Being sarcastic: Take time to consider what you really want and need to say, then be direct.
14. Being critical and/or gossipy: Go directly to the person with whom you have an issue and discuss it. Commit to looking for things worthy of praise and appreciation. Use your words to bless, heal, and improve others.
15. Stuffing hurts: Discuss feelings directly with the person who hurt you.
16. Being passive-aggressive: Learn to be direct and honest about your feelings. Also choose to value yourself equally with others.
17. Withdrawing: Learn to let the other person know why you are withdrawing, the conditions necessary for return, and then commit to return. Ratchet up the length of time you are gone for each time someone says or does something hurtful to you.
18. Shutting down: Request a time-out to give yourself time to think or journal, then commit to discussing the situation later.
19. Experiencing chaos: List what you want to accomplish, prioritize obligations, and decide what's most important. Let go of the less important items, and focus on one task until it is complete.
20. Playing the victim: Figure out what you can do about your situation, then take action.
21. Wanting to self-harm: Seek help, name the fears, and combat the lies driven by those fears.

FROM THE OTHERS-FOCUSED DITCH TO THE ROAD: SESSION 1

Chapters 13 and 14, both of which are divided into three sessions, provide tools to ditch unhealthy behaviors and ponder what you'd like to do instead as you move forward. In session 1 we will concentrate on Others-Focused Ditch Behaviors: sections 1–7.

I've found the do-over to be invaluable in this process.[1] The minute I recognize a ditchy doing, I ask for a do-over and apologize for my unhealthy first try. That way I can practice the better way in real time. Others appreciate that I caught myself, and it helps to establish the new behavior.

A. What hesitations do you have about do-overs, if any?

B. List the positives and negatives about do-overs.

Now we are going to think about some alternative behaviors that can replace the ditchy ways. This takes pressure off in the moment when we tend to resort to that behavior and our mind draws a blank. In this chapter and the next, we are going to create a storehouse of options that we can refer to until we have mastered our on-the-road behaviors and ditched our old ways for good. It may be helpful to write the strategies that work for you in your notebook or journal, then tab the important directives so you can quickly refer to them when needed.

Also, when you realize after the fact that you resorted to a Ditch Behavior (even two weeks later), it is beneficial to review what happened, then think about what you will do differently next time a similar situation arises. That prepares your brain for the future and helps you gain traction. Remember to not be harsh or critical with yourself for resorting to the old behavior. That only bogs you down. Big change happens in small increments. Look for the small changes!

Okay, here we go with figuring out what to do instead of the Others-Focused Ditch Behaviors. Refer to the fears you named in chapter 3, then look in chapter 16 for what options may combat those fears.

1. People-Pleasing

A. What do you gain by people-pleasing?

B. What do you want from others by people-pleasing?

C. What are some ways you can please others and still take yourself into consideration?

2. Default Answer *Yes*

A. What phrase(s) can you use to give yourself time to think before automatically saying yes?

B. If you say yes and then later decide you answered too quickly, what are a couple of statements you can use to backtrack?

3. Readily Giving Up What I Want

A. What are the lies you tell yourself that cause you to give up what you want?

B. What are some truths that can counter those lies?

C. What are some things you can do to pursue things you want to do even if key people aren't interested in doing them?

4. Difficulty Making Decisions

A. What are your roadblocks to making decisions?

B. What can you do to overcome those roadblocks?

5. **Walking on Eggshells**
A. What do you want to communicate?

B. How can you state what needs to be said in a better way?

6. **Difficulty Expressing Feelings or Opinions**
A. What are some feelings you need to confirm for yourself instead of waiting and hoping someone else will validate them for you?

B. What are three small steps you can take to help you develop the ability to share those things that have been kept hidden but need to be spoken?

7. **Avoiding Conflict**
A. What topics do you tend to avoid discussing?

B. What skills might you need to develop to help you express yourself in those areas?

C. What is one step you will take to begin facing those difficult subjects?

**Is there anything you would like to put in your container? If so, do it now.
Feel free to make a note of what you put away.**

Feeling more empowered? I hope so! You've identified strategies to address two-thirds of Others-Focused Ditch Behaviors!

My prayer over you:
Dear God, I pray for this dear reader as they learn to relate in much healthier ways. Help them be patient with themselves and those around them as they work toward incorporating these new methods into their lives. In Jesus' name, amen.

Conversation starters with God:
Now it's your turn to pray. Find a quiet place. Bring a journal and pen if you enjoy writing your prayers. Above all, be prepared to listen to what God has to say to you in response. And because prayer is a conversation with someone who knows and loves you, here are a few conversations starters to get the ball rolling:

Dear God,
- What do You most want for me to take away from today's session?
- Reveal to me which of the behaviors You would like me to focus on first. What do You want me to do about it?
- Half the time I don't have a clue about what I really want. How do I figure that out?
- Learning to speak up is super hard. Show me the safest person with whom to practice.
- I'm so afraid of rejection. How do I survive if people reject me?

Points to ponder in group discussion or private journaling:
1. As you interacted with God, what did you hear from Him?

2. What was the biggest aha moment from this section?

3. Based on what you learned in this session, identify one action you can take that would be helpful.

FROM THE OTHERS-FOCUSED DITCH TO THE ROAD: SESSION 2

In this section we will continue building our arsenal of tools with which to ditch unhealthy behaviors. We will also identify strategies to employ as you move forward. In this session, we will continue with Others-Focused Ditch Behaviors: numbers 8–14.

Refer back to the fears you named in chapter 3, then reread chapter 16 for options to address the fears.

8. Codependence

A. What aspects of "What do other people think of me?" worry you?

B. To what degree (0–100) do you believe God will never leave or forsake you?

C. What steps do you need to take to become interdependent instead of codependent?

9. **Blaming**
   A. We covered this in chapter 12. If you'd like to pick a different situation than you worked through in last chapter, please do so. Or you can skip to number 10, "Being Passive."

   B. Name the situation and the people who are the most responsible for your predicament:

   C. Identify your part (your responsibility) for the circumstances you are now in.

   D. Apologize for your role and forgive yourself. How would you state your apology?

   E. What's the other person's responsibility?

Work toward forgiving them for how they hurt you.

F. What are some options for resolving the issue?

10. Being Passive

A. What do you really want in the situation in which you're being passive?

B. What things/topics do you truly care about?

Work on pursuing those things, keeping others in mind as well to find win-win solutions.

C. What's one step in the direction of taking action instead of remaining passive?

11. Feeling Obligated

A. Is the task you feel obligated to do something that only *you* can do?

B. What can you do about the fears you may have of delegating that task?

C. What are the pros and cons of fulfilling that obligation?

D. Sometimes choosing to fulfill a duty is the best decision. Other times letting go of the obligation or leaving the task to someone else makes more sense. What methods can you employ to ensure that you have chosen wisely?

12. Being Resentful
A. What causes you to feel resentful?

B. What steps can you take to begin to let go of that resentment?

13. Being Sarcastic

A. When is sarcasm okay to use, and when is it a Ditch Behavior?

B. How can you say what needs to be said in a more direct way?

C. Who (include yourself) do you need to work on forgiving?

14. Being Critical and/or Gossipy

A. With whom have you been critical?

B. In what ways have you been guilty of the same or similar things for which you criticized others?

C. When we're in a negative place, it may be difficult to find something praiseworthy, but there's always something to discover, even if it is small or seemingly hidden. What can you praise that person for?

D. Whom have you gossiped about in the last month?

E. List some times you've masked gossip by sharing a "prayer request?"

F. What are ways you can shift the criticism/gossip to words of blessing, healing, and prospering?

> **Is there anything you would like to put in your container? If so, do it now. Feel free to make a note of what you put away.**

My prayer over you:

Dear God, I pray for this dear reader as they practice responding in these new ways. Help them notice their growing confidence in You to help them, increased self-esteem, and courage to change old ways of relating. In Jesus' name, amen.

Conversation starters with God:

Now it's your turn to pray. Find a quiet place. Bring a journal and pen if you enjoy writing your prayers. Above all, be prepared to listen to what God has to say to you in response. And because prayer is a conversation with someone who knows and loves you, here are a few conversations starters to get the ball rolling:

Dear God,
- What do You most want for me to take away from today's session?
- It really *is* someone else's fault what happened to me, so how do I stop blaming them?
- God, I confess I have hidden fear that You have already abandoned me or will reject me. What evidence can You show me that You won't ever reject or abandon me?
- So often I feel obligated to be the one to take care of things. How can I release those obligations when I really don't want to do them anymore?

Points to ponder in group discussion or private journaling:
1. As you interacted with God, what did you hear from Him?

2. What was the biggest aha moment from this section?

3. Based on what you learned in this session, identify one action you can take that would be helpful.

FROM THE OTHERS-FOCUSED DITCH TO THE ROAD: SESSION 3

In this section we will continue gathering tools for our toolbox to help you ditch unhealthy behaviors. We will also identify strategies to employ as you move forward. In this session, we will continue with Others-Focused Ditch Behaviors: numbers 15–21.

Refer to the fears you named in chapter 3, then look in chapter 16 for options to address the fears.

15. Stuffing Hurts

Beginning to change this pattern could start with journaling how you feel, then sharing in a recovery group where there's little to no risk. Once you have built up confidence, share with the person who hurt you.

A. What is your plan to shift from stuffing your hurts to expressing them in a healthy way?

B. What will your first step be?

16. Being Passive-Aggressive

A. Think of the last time you acted in a passive-aggressive manner. What is a more direct way you could respond in a similar situation in the future?

B. What fears need to be overcome to do this?

17. **Withdrawing**
A. When is it appropriate to withdraw from a situation, and when is leaving a ditchy behavior?

B. What's the reason you're upset? How can you express that in a direct and beneficial manner?

C. How can you withdraw in a healthy way and convey to the other person why you are leaving?

D. Is your situation physically unsafe for you and/or your children? If yes, get help to remove yourself, then assess how to improve it or leave it permanently.

Who can help you?

18. Shutting Down

When we shut down, we're flooded emotionally and can't respond in the moment.

A. How will you request time to gather your thoughts and process what's going on?

B. After you've had time to think, what is a better way to express what you were thinking and feeling? Some options could be via a letter, a one-to-one conversation (with another person present), or with a counselor:

19. Experiencing Chaos

A. What areas of your life feel chaotic?

B. What are three steps you can take to reduce the amount of chaos in your life?

20. Playing the Victim

A. In what situations have you felt victimized?

B. What can you do to change those circumstances?

21. Wanting to Self-Harm

When we reach this point, we are feeling extremely powerless. It doesn't seem that *anything* can be done to improve the situation.

A. Identify the behavior(s) that cause self-harm.

B. What negative things are you telling yourself?

C. What are the fears that are swirling around?

D. Look at chapter 16 and list three things you can do about your situation despite how hopeless it may feel.

> **Is there anything you would like to put in your container? If so, do it now. Feel free to make a note of what you put away.**

If working through any of the above Ditch Behaviors seems insurmountable, seeking the help of a professional life coach or counselor would be money well spent. If you are financially strapped, do an Internet search on "low-cost counseling." The mistakes we make through Ditch Behaviors can be more costly than counseling as we experience failed relationships, poor decisions, and addictions from trying to cope with the pain of being in the ditch.

That was a lot to think about! The more we focus on this, the easier it gets. As you know well by now, healing is a process. We've circled back a couple of times to these Ditch Behaviors in our journey out of the ditch.

In what ways is life getting better since you've been going through this study? Or maybe it seems worse! Remember in chapter 8 when we talked about the process of change? It may be because you now know your old behaviors don't work, but you haven't yet internalized the new ones. Remember: *that is change!* We're just not at our destination yet! Keep at it! It will most assuredly pay off.

My prayer over you:

Dear God, I pray for this dear reader as they may feel like the journey is so long and hard. Encourage this reader and reassure them this is the right path. With Your help they can do this. Help them achieve their goals and experience deeper joy in their lives. Thank You for being with them this whole way. In Jesus' name, amen.

Conversation starters with God:

Now it's your turn to pray. Find a quiet place. Bring a journal and pen if you enjoy writing your prayers. Above all, be prepared to listen to what God has to say to you in response. And because prayer is a conversation with someone who knows and loves you, here are a few conversations starters to get the ball rolling:

Dear God,
- What do You most want for me to take away from today's session?
- How do I begin to unpack all the hurts I carry? It seems such an impossible task. I'm afraid of being overwhelmed. Show me how to do this one little bit at a time.
- My reactions are so ingrained. What do You want me to focus on first?
- It doesn't feel like I have anyone I can turn to. God, show me who I can turn to during my feelings of despair.

Points to ponder in group discussion or private journaling:

1. As you interacted with God, what did you hear from Him?

2. What was the biggest aha moment from this section?

3. Based on what you learned in this session, identify one action you can take that would be helpful.

CHAPTER 14

FROM THE ME-FOCUSED DITCH TO THE ROAD

Read or reread chapter 14 in Unstuck.

Main Ideas

Here is a list of the main ideas you'll find in chapter 14:

Following, in a nutshell, are suggestions for overcoming the MF Ditch Behaviors:

1. Being selfish: Take into consideration what others want as well, as what you want, and learn to balance those. Learn to give.
2. Defaulting to *no*: Give yourself time to think before answering, and allow yourself to change your no to yes.
3. Being a perfectionist: Decide that your best *is* good enough. You don't have to be perfect to be loved. Strive for and celebrate excellence instead.
4. Needing to be right: Get rid of the pride of being right, develop a humble attitude, and recognize there's always a chance that you are wrong.
5. Having difficulty seeing others' perspectives: Recognize this tendency, and decide to value the perspectives of others even if you disagree. Their perspectives enhance your viewpoint; they don't invalidate it.
6. Demanding: Change wording of demands to requests. Refer to "Turn Your Words to Gold."[1]
7. Manipulating: Develop a more direct approach in requesting what you want.
8. Criticizing: Consciously choose to look for the good. Accept that God fully loves and accepts you. Start loving and accepting yourself and others despite faults and imperfections.

9. Controlling: We only have control over what we <u>D</u>o; our <u>A</u>ttitude, <u>R</u>esponse, <u>T</u>houghts; and what we <u>S</u>ay (DARTS). Concentrate on controlling those.
10. Being vocal about feelings and wants: Remember to draw out the thoughts and feelings of others that may differ from your viewpoint. Listen seeking to understand others.
11. Having high expectations: Become conscious of hidden expectations, and express what you want to have happen.
12. Being disappointed: Understand and evaluate your expectations. Change the meaning you attach to others not living up to your expectations.
13. Being angry: Identify your underlying fears and choose to resolve them.
14. Demeaning behaviors: Address the deep-seated insecurities or hatred you feel, and consciously choose to act in loving ways. Solid rock security comes from trusting in God. Identify what areas you need to grow in faith.
15. Threatening behaviors: Identify where the powerless feeling comes from, name the fear, then brainstorm and figure out what to do differently.
16. Yelling: Take a time-out to acknowledge fears and identify other options. Learn how to express what you want in an empowered way.
17. Attacking and accusing: Identify what you want, and take responsibility for your part in the issue.
18. Being rigid: Identify the fears hidden under strict rules, then ask God to reveal how to remain both safe and flexible at the same time.
19. Becoming addicted: Seek counseling and attend a recovery group. Naming and addressing the fears driving the addiction can help set you free. Also, learn and develop better communication skills.
20. Physically attacking: Seek God's help and counseling to reveal and heal imbedded fears and emotional issues. Take a time-out when you feel triggered to find out what's driving your behaviors and develop a plan to change those behaviors.
21. Harming others: Seek help from God, counseling, and recovery groups to stop the cycle of harm. Recognize that fear of facing the past keeps you imprisoned and enslaved to behaviors that make you hate yourself.

FROM THE ME-FOCUSED DITCH TO THE ROAD: SESSION 1

In this chapter we examine how to get out of Me-Focused Ditch Behaviors and onto the road. Remember the idea of do-overs we talked about at the beginning of chapter 13? They provide real-time practice in life and help us progress more rapidly. Continue to be kind to yourself as you are working on these changes, and commit to helping each other in a kind way to ditch those old, ineffective ways of reacting.

We will now consider replacement options for those ditchy behaviors we find in the Me-Focused Ditch. That way you'll be prepared with alternatives when you need them, or after the fact when you review what happened. Remember, these ditchy behaviors were the model you were shown growing up—from your ancestors, parents, teachers, family members, and the media. They are deeply ingrained in each of us.

Refer to the fears you named in chapter 3, then revisit chapter 16 for options to address the fears.

1. Selfish

A. On what topics do you tend to think only of what you want?

B. What has been the effect when you got what you wanted and disregarded the wants and needs of others?

C. Name three places you can give of your time, money, or resources instead of getting. Think of interests you have and what's important to you, then do something to help provide that for someone else.

2. Default Answer *No*

A. Until you have a chance to think about the question, what can you say to yourself or others when they ask something of you and your automatic answer would typically be no?

B. If you said no, then reconsidered, what can you say to the person to whom you previously told no?

3. Perfectionist

A. Define what "good enough" means to you.

Often, our subconscious definition translates to "good enough means better than my best could ever be." Is that true for you? Yes _____ No _____

It is if you're disappointed with your work, even though you gave it your best effort.

B. What can you do to combat the fears connected to not being perfect?

4. Need to Be Right
A. What do you tell yourself when you are not right?

B. What are some options for combatting those lies?

C. What would it cost you to let go of the need to be right?

5. Difficulty Seeing Others' Perspectives
A. In what areas and topics do you have difficulty seeing the perspective of others?

B. What keeps you from seeing the other person's viewpoint? What fears come up as a result?

C. What are three steps you can take to begin combating seeing only through your own eyes?

6. Demanding
A. What is not happening that you want to have happen?

B. How can you state what you want in a way that's empowering to you? (Refer to https://www.loveandlogic.com/pages/turn-your-word-into-gold)

7. Manipulative
A. When you are acting in a manipulative way, what does it look like? (For example: flirting, begging, pleading, guilting, tantrums, coercion, etc.)

B. What is a more direct way of stating what you want?

Is there anything you would like to put in your container? If so, do it now. Feel free to make a note of what you put away.

We're one-third the way through Me-Focused Behaviors! Yeah! Life will be so much better for you down the road as you apply these strategies. Take a moment to congratulate yourself on the hard work you're doing.

My prayer over you:

Dear God, I pray for this dear reader as they come up with ideas and a plan for changing from ditchy ways of living. Help them feel better about themselves as they do this. In Jesus' name, amen.

Conversation starters with God:

Now it's your turn to pray. Find a quiet place. Bring a journal and pen if you enjoy writing your prayers. Above all, be prepared to listen to what God has to say to you in response. And because prayer is a conversation with someone who knows and loves you, here are a few conversations starters to get the ball rolling:

Dear God,
- What do You most want for me to take away from today's session?
- It's so important for me to be perfect and right. How can I relax my standards and still experience excellence?
- Show me how to change my automatic no answer and instead say, "Let me think about it and get back to you."
- How do I get people to comply without manipulating and demanding?

Points to ponder in group discussion or private journaling:
1. As you interacted with God, what did you hear from Him?

2. What was the biggest aha moment from this section?

3. Based on what you learned in this session, identify one action you can take that would be helpful.

FROM THE ME-FOCUSED DITCH TO THE ROAD: SESSION 2

We're going to continue identifying replacement options for those ditchy behaviors we find on the Me-Focused side. In this session, we examine behaviors 8–14. You will be preparing alternatives for when you need them, or to review when you remember you engaged in Ditch Behaviors.

Refer to the fears you named in chapter 3, then examine chapter 16 for options to address the fears.

8. Criticizing

A. Who do you tend to criticize?

B. What can you do about the fears you listed in chapter 3 about criticizing?

C. Whatever we focus on becomes bigger. What good do you see in the people you have criticized?

D. Jot down two positive compliments you could make for a person you listed above.

E. Look for times when the individual does what you want them to do, then compliment them on the parts they did to your satisfaction, even if it's not exactly perfect.

9. Controlling
A. In what ways do you feel out of control?

B. What situations do you feel you need to control?

Think of one situation you tend to try to control, then apply DARTS (Do, Attitude, Respond, Think, Say). How can you respond differently for each letter of the acronym?
Do:

Attitude:

Respond:

Think:

Say:

C. What can you do about the fears listed in chapter 3 related to the need to be in control of situations or others?

10. Vocal About Feelings and Wants
A. It's not wrong to be vocal about thoughts and feelings, but in what ways does that shut down others who aren't as forceful about the topic (example: Politics or Religion)?

B. What topics do you tend to be vocal about?

C. What can you do to prevent shutting others down?

11. High Expectations
A. In what areas of your life do you have high expectations of yourself or others?

B. Were the expectations clearly stated? If yes, did the other party wholeheartedly agree or passively agree?

C. How can you rephrase and restate your expectations in a "turn-your-words-to-gold" way? Refer to https://www.loveandlogic.com/pages/turn-your-word-into-gold:[3]

D. What can you do to overcome the fears noted in chapter 3 that underlie high expectations?

12. Disappointment

A. Describe a recent time when you felt disappointed.

B. What did you hope would happen that didn't?

C. What meaning did you attach to that experience?
(Examples: "I can never get what I want." Or "No one listens to me.")

D. What steps can you take to let go of the way you expect things to be and accept things as they are instead?

13. Being Angry

A. What recent event or person made you angry?

B. What were the fears underlying the situation?

C. What can you do to resolve those fears?

14. Demeaning

A. Give an example of when you've talked to someone in a contemptuous, belittling, or an "I'm better than you" way (consider when you've used a harsh tone too).

B. How did you feel about it after reflecting on the situation?

C. What can you do to resolve the contempt you feel for that person or those people?

D. In what ways do you have contempt toward yourself?

E. Outline three steps toward forgiving yourself and others for the things that bother you.

> **Is there anything you would like to put in your container? If so, do it now.
> Feel free to make a note of what you put away.**

My prayer over you:

Dear God, I pray for this dear reader as they work through the process of identifying alternative ways of responding. Help them notice the growing internal strength and confidence that comes with responding instead of reacting. Dissipate their anger and replace it with feelings of peace. In Jesus' name, amen.

Conversation starters with God:

Now it's your turn to pray. Find a quiet place. Bring a journal and pen if you enjoy writing your prayers. Above all, be prepared to listen to what God has to say to you in response. And because prayer is a conversation with someone who knows and loves you, here are a few conversations starters to get the ball rolling:

Dear God,
- What do You most want for me to take away from today's session?
- What hidden expectations keep sabotaging my life with disappointments?
- Show me where the roots of my anger lie. Where can I turn to get help with this?
- Where does my tendency to be demeaning show up?
- What pain am I hiding behind that attitude?

Points to ponder in group discussion or private journaling:

1. As you interacted with God, what did you hear from Him?

2. What was the biggest aha moment from this section?

3. Based on what you learned in this session, identify one action you can take that would be helpful.

FROM THE ME-FOCUSED DITCH TO THE ROAD: SESSION 3

This session is the last segment of Me-Focused Behaviors: sections 15–21. We continue the process of listing replacement options for the ditchy behaviors we find on the Me-Focused side. You are preparing and accumulating alternatives for when you need them.

Refer to the fears you named in chapter 3, then refer to chapter 16 for options to address the fears.

15. Threatening

A. What types of threats have been made toward you or that you have you made toward others?

B. List common situations in which you find yourself resorting to threats to get others to do what you want:

C. Instead of threatening, what benefit(s) will you offer an individual for accomplishing the task you desire?

D. How can you revise your wording in a "turn-your-words-to-gold" way? See the link in the notes for guidance.[4]

16. Yelling

A. What can you do about the fears causing you to resort to yelling?

B. Name three ways you can respond in a different way or buy yourself time to cool down instead of yelling.

17. Attacking / Accusing

A. Consider a situation in which you have attacked, accused, told another what they needed to do, or asserted that what they did was wrong. Write down how you can express your feelings and say what you want in a healthier way. (Refer to chapter 11 for help.)

B. What can you say when you catch yourself attacking or accusing to let someone know you'd like to change what you just said?

18. Rigid

A. On what topics do you tend to be unbending, strict, or a rule follower?

B. What are the fears related to rigidity?

C. What are three strategies for overcoming those fears?

D. If you have difficulty identifying the underlying fears, ask God to reveal them. Write the impression you got from God.

19. Addict

A. What are your addictions or obsessive-compulsive behaviors?

B. What emotionally or physically painful thoughts, feelings, or situations you are desiring to escape?

C. What are three strategies to help you shift the tendency to turn to some repetitive or mind-numbing behavior? (Socially acceptable actions tend to be work, exercise, cleaning, serving others, or being thin. Socially frowned upon behaviors are drug and alcohol use, gambling, pornography, or extramarital sex, to name a few.)

20. Physical Attacks

A. Think of a time you physically attacked someone or were involved in a fight (even if you have to go back to childhood to find an example).

B. If you can remember, what led up to the fight?

C. Think about how you felt when you engaged in the fight. What were you trying to defend?

D. What are three things you can you do to overcome the powerlessness you felt in those circumstances?

21. Harming Others

A. Jot down a couple of instances in which you harmed someone else either with words or deeds.

B. Think about the shame and guilt that you felt, and write about what drove you to do or say what you did.

C. Outline a plan and steps to take to begin shifting that pattern. Getting help with this may be the best gift you could give yourself and your family this year.

D. What is the first step you're going to take?

The website LoveandLogic.com offers additional resources and a number of articles to help in challenging situations.

There is power in taking a time-out to allow yourself time to think of a more effective response. It takes a lot of courage and mental energy to choose a different path than following the model you received growing up.

Completing these last two chapters constitutes a major milestone. What will you do to celebrate this deep and very meaningful work?

> **Is there anything you would like to put in your container? If so, do it now. Feel free to make a note of what you put away.**

Whew! That was hard to write, and even harder to think about those behaviors and how they apply to daily life. I know in my life, for each of the above behaviors there was something I could think of that I was guilty of doing. That's big growth in my awareness from less than ten years ago when I didn't think I was Me-Focused at all! I have so much more freedom now because I've worked through the fears that drove my own Me-Focused and Others-Focused Ditch Behaviors. That is my desire for you too. However, I know this is a *lot* of work! So take as much time as you need. I think that's why God gives us a lifetime to learn. He knows we can't change all these things at once.

My prayer over you:

Dear God, I pray for this dear reader as they experience a deeper realization of how much we all need a Savior to rescue us from these ways of reacting. Please help them let go of being critical and condemning of themselves for their mistakes and failures. Help them notice ways they are improving. Help them remember to ask for help every day, especially for those things they feel powerless to stop. In Jesus' name, amen.

Conversation starters with God:

Now it's your turn to pray. Find a quiet place. Bring a journal and pen if you enjoy writing your prayers. Above all, be prepared to listen to what God has to say

to you in response. And because prayer is a conversation with someone who knows and loves you, here are a few conversations starters to get the ball rolling:

Dear God,
- What do You most want for me to take away from today's session?
- Recall any other situations You want me to address when I yelled, attacked, accused, or threatened. I hate it when someone does that to me, and I want to eliminate that from my life. When has that happened?
- What behaviors do You want me to become aware of that I have used to distract myself from how powerless I have felt?
- What boundaries do I need to set with others when they yell, attack, accuse, or threaten me?

Points to ponder in group discussion or private journaling:

1. As you interacted with God, what did you hear from Him?

2. What was the biggest aha moment from this section?

3. Based on what you learned in this session, identify one action you can take that would be helpful.

CHAPTER 15

ON THE ROAD

Read or reread chapter 15 in *Unstuck*.

Main Ideas

Here's a list of the ideas you'll find in chapter 15:
1. The road represents consciousness, balance, mindfulness, and awareness.
2. When we are "on the road," we are able to balance our wants and needs with those of others.
3. When we are "on the road," we are free from trying to control others. We are also in the best position to help others out of their ditches when they are ready to seek assistance.
4. We are either influenced by the invisible promptings of God or by negative forces of the enemy, which manifest as ditch behaviors.
5. We learn to live "on the road" by listening to the promptings of the Holy Spirit and allowing the invisible inspiration of God to influence our everyday actions.
6. Being Others-Focused has strengths, some of which include deeply caring for others, being easygoing, flexible, spontaneous, adventurous, generous, hospitable, and a supportive follower.
7. Being Me-Focused has strengths, some of which include being goal-oriented, driven, motivated, focused, a good leader, being creative, single-minded, and striving for excellence.
8. Because we spent time in both ditches, we can reap the benefits of both Others-Focused and Me-Focused characteristics.

ON THE ROAD: SESSION 1

The focus of *Unstuck* is to get out of the ditch and onto the road, which is where we want to be most of the time. There are some important things to consider that can help keep you on the road once you get there. This is the fun chapter where you get to look at what you've been doing well and want to continue.

1. In which areas of your life do you feel like you are the most balanced and on the road?

2. How much would you say your consciousness has grown as a result of this study?

3. To what degree would you say your mindfulness (both of what you want and what others want) has improved?

4. Rate the level of awareness you have now compared to what it was when you first started this study on a scale of 0–10, with 10 being "complete awareness."

5. What are some ways you can grow in submitting to God to allow His Spirit, the invisible, to move the visible of what goes on in your life?

6. How much less fear and anxiety would you say you have now?

7. What strengths have you gained from time spent in the Others-Focused Ditch?

8. What abilities have you acquired from the Me-Focused Ditch?

9. What strengths do you think should be added to the Others-Focused side?

10. What strengths do you think should be added to the Me-Focused side?

God encourages us to keep our focus on the positive. Philippians 4:8 urges us to meditate on the following things: "Whatever things are true, whatever things are noble, whatever things are just, whatever things are pure, whatever things are lovely, whatever things are of good report, if there is any virtue and if there is anything praiseworthy—meditate on these things."

We want to keep these categories in mind as we evaluate our own thoughts about ourselves. How many of us maintain a running commentary in our heads, focusing on what we did well and that which was lovely, noble, just, pure, and praiseworthy?

I'd venture to bet most of us don't. But we can cultivate that. If we meditate on these things, remembering that God is the one who made all those things possible in our lives and giving Him praise for it, we prevent ourselves from becoming puffed up and prideful. Keeping our focus on the good in the midst of all the bad around us fills us with joy, peace, and happiness. Do you want that for your life?

My prayer over you:

Dear God, I pray for this dear reader as they turn their focus on the positive: the good work You are doing in their life, and the ways You've made their life better. Thank you for the growth and balance You bring to their lives. Bring my readers joy and peace. In Jesus' name, amen.

Conversation starters with God:

Now it's your turn to pray. Find a quiet place. Bring a journal and pen if you enjoy writing your prayers. Above all, be prepared to listen to what God has to say to you in response. And because prayer is a conversation with someone who knows and loves you, here are a few conversations starters to get the ball rolling:

Dear God,
- What do You most want for me to take away from today's session?
- Where are the strengths You gave me?
- Bring to mind things I do that come naturally or easily for me. Help me to recognize those as strengths.
- I have a tendency to focus on what's wrong with me. God, please show me the good You see in me.

Points to ponder in group discussion or private journaling:
1. As you interacted with God, what did you hear from Him?

2. What was the biggest aha moment from this section?

3. Based on what you learned in this session, identify one action you can take that would be helpful.

CHAPTER 16

WHAT TO DO ABOUT FEAR

Read or reread chapter 16 in *Unstuck*.

Main Ideas

Here's a list of the main ideas you'll find in chapter 16.
Below are twenty-four ways to tackle fear:

1. Pray about it.
2. Talk about it, then ask for input from others.
3. Brainstorm for new options; evaluate what works best.
4. Make a list of pros and cons for each option.
5. Identify the lie, accept the piece that is true, and reject the rest.
6. Identify the lie and counter with the truth.
7. Change your story.
8. Figure out what you can do, then do it.
9. Reprioritize.
10. Face the fear and do it anyway.
11. Identify the extremes and figure out what is in between.
12. If you can't do anything about it, decide to let it go.
13. Learn or educate yourself about the topic.
14. "I can do all things through Christ who strengthens me" (Philippians 4:13).
15. Look at it from God's perspective.
16. Remember that in the end, the situation will turn out for the best.
17. Ask yourself: "What is the worst-case scenario, and how likely is that to happen?"

18. Use coping skills to calm down.
19. Ask yourself: "How could this be worse?"
20. Journal about it.
21. Do EFT (Emotional Freedom Technique) on it.
22. Go to counseling.
23. Attend a recovery group.
24. In the name of Jesus, cast it out.

WHAT TO DO ABOUT FEAR: SESSION 1

This chapter may be the most important in this whole book! Here, we find twenty-four ways of addressing fears and powerless feelings. This chapter has been divided into four sessions to allow ample time to process each of the questions. You may want to write general answers in this workbook and respond more specifically to a particular situation in your notebook or journal. I hope you will turn to this chapter time and again to aid you in combating the daily onslaught of fears.

Formula:
1. Name the ditchy behavior.
2. Identify the fear(s) driving the behavior.
3. Refer to chapter 16 in *Unstuck* for ideas on overcoming the fear(s).
4. Take the necessary action.
5. Repeat as new situations and fears arise.

For each of the following twenty-four methods of addressing fear, it is helpful to consider which options apply best to various situations:

1. Pray about it.
As a believer, this is a no-brainer. So let's take a deeper look.
A. About which issues do you consistently turn to God?

B. What kinds of situations have overwhelmed you in the past?

C. When did you think to pray about those things?

D. Are you facing any situations in which you feel powerless to create a change? If yes, what are they?

From 1 Corinthians 4:10, pray the "I'm powerless to make anything happen" prayer. Confess, "When I am weak, God is strong," then wait until God intervenes. Keep a journal of what happens along the way.

2. Talk about it. Get input from others.

A. What dilemma are you facing?

B. What questions do you have about the situation?

C. Where do you feel stuck?

D. To whom do you go for wisdom and insight?

E. If you don't have anyone, to whom could you consider turning in the future?

F. Who can you trust to keep what you share confidential?

G. Who has been through something similar in which you desire the kind of outcome they achieved?

H. Whose judgment do you trust?

I. If it has to do with a conflict with someone, write out a draft of what you might say. Read it to someone else to check if your words bring up defensive reactions. Make changes, then approach the person with whom you have the conflict, using your prepared message.[1]

3. Brainstorm for new options. Evaluate what works best.

This option proves to be helpful for a wide variety of situations. It can help us determine where to go on vacation, create a reference list of "what to do for fun," come up with potential solutions to problems, and decide on a course of action. Thinking of every possible option "nips in the bud" the fear of making a wrong decision. Remember, write down *all* ideas, whether they seem ridiculous or not.

What kinds of situations might lend themselves well to brainstorming for you?

4. Make a list and rate the pros and cons for each option that holds merit.

A. When have you used this approach before?

B. How was it helpful?

C. On what upcoming decisions could you utilize this?

5. Identify the lie, accept the piece that is true, and reject the rest.

A. What are some things people have said that were very hurtful to you?

B. What part of what they said was not true?

C. What part is true?

Even though it hurts admitting a fault or failure, acknowledging it promotes awareness. That empowers us to make different and better choices going forward. We can also make a conscious decision to let go of the feeling of shame that comes with that because God will remove our shame. Isaiah 61:7 tells us, "Instead of your shame you shall have double honor."

6. Identify the lie and counter with the truth.
This is similar to number 5, but in this case it's more about the lies we are telling ourselves. They are more long-standing and may have come from what we heard growing up: "You idiot!" "Can't you do anything right?" Or they might be what we concluded because of childhood experiences: "I'm not good enough" or "I have to be perfect."

A. What are some of the lies you have been believing and repeating over and over in your mind?

B. With which truths can you counter those lies? If it's difficult to find a truth, ask for input from others.

You have just completed the first of four segments of this chapter. This preparation work will help you more effectively deal with problems going forward. It's exciting to be empowered!

My prayer over you:

Dear God, I pray for this dear reader as they gain tools to help with challenges they will face. Help them remember to refer to this information as often as needed until it's internalized. In Jesus' name, amen.

Conversation starters with God:

Now it's your turn to pray. Find a quiet place. Bring a journal and pen if you enjoy writing your prayers. Above all, be prepared to listen to what God has to say to you in response. And because prayer is a conversation with someone who knows and loves you, here are a few conversations starters to get the ball rolling:

Dear God,
- What do You most want for me to take away from today's session?
- What things have I failed to pray because I felt so powerless that I didn't think there was anything You could do either?
- What lies have I been telling myself over and over that keep me from becoming the person You created me to be?

Points to ponder in group discussion or private journaling:

1. As you interacted with God, what did you hear from Him?

2. What was the biggest aha moment from this section?

3. Based on what you learned in this session, identify one action you can take that would be helpful.

WHAT TO DO ABOUT FEAR: SESSION 2

We continue exploring ways to overcome anxieties by examining more closely each of the twenty-four strategies for addressing fear.

7. Change your story.
A. Some of the things I used to tell myself were: "I'll never get what I want." "Nobody loves me." "I'm a victim." What stories do you tell yourself because of your past experiences?

B. What new story would you like to tell yourself going forward?

8. Figure out what you can do, then do it.
A. In what situation do you feel stuck right now?

Maybe you'll need to employ several other options to come up with an action plan. For example, pray about it, talk about it with others, brainstorm for solutions, and look at pros and cons.

B. List one step you can take to begin to get unstuck from this situation.

9. Reprioritize if necessary.

A. Make a list of all the things you need to do.

B. Now review that list and rate each item according to the deadline by which it must be accomplished. You may wish to do this on a separate piece of paper.

C. Choose the one you rated number 1 and start working on that, ignoring the rest until that task is completed.

D. How is your stress level affected by having an action plan?

10. Face the fear and do it anyway.

A. What have you done that was scary or terrifying, but you did it anyway?

B. What did it feel like after you did what you were so afraid of doing?

C. I'm assuming you felt great, exhilarated, or satisfied. If that wasn't the outcome, what happened instead?

D. In what ways does a negative experience make it even harder to face a fear and do it anyway?

E. What can you do to overcome that fear?

11. Identify the extremes and figure out what is in between.
A. Think of a situation in which you feel stuck. What are the extremes?
(Examples: Keep quiet or yell at someone. Get a divorce or stay unhappily married.)

B. What are some options in between your extremes?

12. If you can't do anything about it, decide to let it go.

A. Besides getting stuck in traffic or personally running the country, what are some areas in which you have been worrying but have no control of the outcome?

B. Practice making a conscious decision right now to let go of worrying about them.

C. What gets in the way of letting go of the worry?

Figure out what to do about next. Remember, worrying only robs us of peace in the moment. It does nothing to alter the situation. Unload your worries in prayer, then decide that God is powerful enough to handle the situation, even if He isn't acting on your timeline or in the way you hope. That will help set you free.

13. Learn or educate yourself about the topic.

A. Which situations are you facing in which you have no knowledge or experience?

B. Where can you turn to obtain the necessary knowledge to overcome the fear?

C. Name the first step you will take to begin to learn about this new area.

14. Christ gives me the strength to face anything.

A. What big or overwhelming things are you facing right now?

B. To what degree (percentage) do you believe that you can handle this situation through Christ who strengthens you (Philippians 4:13)

C. If your percentage is less than 100, what can you do to grow toward trusting God for the strength you need?

My prayer over you:

Dear God, I pray for this dear reader for You to help them get into the habit of finding, naming, and overcoming their fears. You tell us time and again, "Do not be afraid." Help them to let go of the fears even when they have reason to be afraid. In Jesus' name, amen.

Conversation starters with God:

Now it's your turn to pray. Find a quiet place. Bring a journal and pen if you enjoy writing your prayers. Above all, be prepared to listen to what God has to say to you in response. And because prayer is a conversation with someone who knows and loves you, here are a few conversations starters to get the ball rolling:

Dear God,
- What do You most want for me to take away from today's session?
- You know what's going on in my life right now. Please show me which of these strategies to apply to address the challenges I'm facing.
- Where can I turn to learn about what I need to know to move forward?
- Place just the right person or people in my path to help me with my next step. Who are they?

Points to ponder in group discussion or private journaling:

1. As you interacted with God, what did you hear from Him?

2. What was the biggest aha moment from this section?

3. Based on what you learned in this session, identify one action you can take that would be helpful.

WHAT TO DO ABOUT FEAR: SESSION 3

We're halfway through ways we can overcome fears that bombard us! Let's continue.

15. Look at it from God's perspective.

A. What is God doing in your life through the challenge you are facing?

B. In what ways are you drawing closer to God because of your situation?
    (Examples: praying, studying, fasting, seeking help from others, growing in the fruit of the Spirit (Galatians 5:22–23).

16. Remember that the end of the situation will turn out for the best.

A. When or how will you know it's the end of the situation?

B. In what ways could God be making it work out for the good even in the midst of it feeling really awful, evil, or wrong?

17. Ask yourself: What is the worst-case scenario, and how likely is that to happen?

A. What is the worst-case scenario?

B. How likely is that to happen?

C. What can you do to prepare for or prevent it from happening?

18. Use coping skills to calm down.

A. What things prevent you from dealing with a situation you know needs to be addressed, yet you can't attend to it right now?

B. How are you coping in healthy ways?

C. Are you coping in not-so-healthy ways?

D. From the list of coping options listed on pages 237–238 in *Unstuck*, make up your own list of coping skills for times you need them. Add in any healthy coping skills not mentioned on the list that you have used.
1. What things calm you down?

2. How can you allow time to think about what happened?

3. What methods do you use to distract yourself from the issue?

19. Ask yourself: "How could this be worse?"
A. In what ways could your situation be worse than it is?

B. Send a prayer of thanks that it's not worse than it is. 1 Thessalonians 5:18 says, "In everything give thanks; for this is the will of God in Christ Jesus for you." This is one way to be thankful despite horrible circumstances.

My prayer over you:

Dear God, I pray for this dear reader as You help them develop more ways of dealing with fears and anxieties in life. Help them remember these strategies the next time they are faced with fears. In Jesus' name, amen.

Conversation starters with God:

Now it's your turn to pray. Find a quiet place. Bring a journal and pen if you enjoy writing your prayers. Above all, be prepared to listen to what God has to say to you in response. And because prayer is a conversation with someone who knows and loves you, here are a few conversations starters to get the ball rolling:

Dear God,
- What do You most want for me to take away from today's session?
- What is Your perspective on my suffering and the trials I'm going through and have been through?
- How can I find things to be thankful for amidst my trials? Show me.
- What coping skills are healthy for me, and which ways am I coping that You want me to change?

Points to ponder in group discussion or private journaling:
1. As you interacted with God, what did you hear from Him?

2. What was the biggest aha moment from this section?

3. Based on what you learned in this session, identify one action you can take that would be helpful.

WHAT TO DO ABOUT FEAR: SESSION 4

In this session, we complete our list of options for overcoming fears. Let's dive in.

20. Journal

Writing down what's going on in our heads helps us get out of the broken record or scratched-compact-disc state of mind. Writing gives us something to do when it doesn't feel like there's anything else we can do. Putting words to paper also helps bring clarity to the situation.

A. What has your experience been with journaling?

B. What blocks to journaling do you face?

C. What can you do about those obstacles?

D. What forms of journaling have you tried or are willing to try to help you work through the challenges you're facing right now?

E. What do you need to do to ensure the security of your journal?

21. Do Emotional Freedom Technique (EFT) on it. (www.emofree.com)
A. What do you know about the Emotional Freedom Technique?

B. What barriers do you have in using this tool?

C. What can you do to overcome these blocks?

D. Rate the level of intensity of the issue from 0–10 (10 = the worst). _____
Now do EFT tapping until the intensity reduces to zero. Sometimes this happens rapidly; other times it will slowly go down over time as you keep working on the problem.

22. Go to counseling.
A. What reservations do you have about seeking the help of a therapist?

B. What obstacles keep you from seeking professional help?

C. If you decide to see a counselor or life coach, what do you hope to gain from the experience?

D. To find options for a counselor or life coach in your area, you can check with your local church for recommendations, ask friends, search the Internet for "Christian counselors or coaches near me," or go to PsychologyToday.com and click on the tab "find a therapist." You may wish to identify an issue you want to discuss with the professional before going to your first session.

23. Attend a recovery group.

The thought of attending a recovery group seems daunting to many. It was to me. It felt to me that darkening the door of a recovery group proved that I was a failure. But the truth was, it was a giant step of courage *away* from the failure I already experienced in my life. I found community and understanding for the first time, which helped me find freedom.

A. What issues are most prevalent in your life that might improve through attending a recovery group?

B. What obstacles stand in your way of attending?

C. What goal would you like to set for yourself related to attending a recovery group?

24. In the name of Jesus, cast it out.
Every person on this planet is bombarded by a host of fears daily. It doesn't mean you are possessed if you are afraid. At the same time, 2 Timothy 1:7 says, "God has not given us a spirit of fear." That means fear is a spirit and did not come from God. So we have the power to command it to leave. It has the power to stay, though, if we unwittingly agree with or allow the fear.

A. What fears are you afraid to let go because they've been with you as long as you can remember?

B. What thoughts go through your head about the idea of casting out fears by telling them to go away in the name of Jesus?

C. What happened when you told the fear to go away in Jesus' name?

D. If it didn't leave, you may need some help to discover what gives the fear the right to stay.

E. Which of the above ways of overcoming fear had you already mastered before going through this study guide?

F. What is one fear you want to focus on overcoming?

This concludes the twenty-four ways of addressing fear. Perhaps you have other methods not listed here. If so, I'd love to hear about them so I can include that information in future versions. Getting rid of fear is about learning to trust God in those areas in which fear exists. It's a process. We don't get there overnight. Be patient with yourself as you work on these things. God gave us a whole lifetime for a reason.

My prayer over you:
Dear God, I pray for this dear reader as they implement new ways of fighting off Satan's fear attacks. Give them the courage and perseverance to continue the battle and grow deeper in trusting You in all areas of their lives. In Jesus' name, amen.

Conversation starters with God:

Now it's your turn to pray. Find a quiet place. Bring a journal and pen if you enjoy writing your prayers. Above all, be prepared to listen to what God has to say to you in response. And because prayer is a conversation with someone who knows and loves you, here are a few conversations starters to get the ball rolling:

Dear God,
- What do You most want for me to take away from today's session?
- What are You prompting me to do next in my healing journey?
- If You want me to get help, please impress on my mind where to seek that help. Help me find just the right person or group that will help me grow. Where do You want me to look?

Points to ponder in group discussion or private journaling:

1. As you interacted with God, what did you hear from Him?

2. What was the biggest aha moment from this section?

3. Based on what you learned in this session, identify one action you can take that would be helpful.

CHAPTER 17

DEVELOPING AN IDEAL RELATIONSHIP

Read or reread chapter 17 in Unstuck.

Main Ideas

Here is a list of the main ideas you'll find in chapter 17:

We increase the chances of developing an ideal relationship when we have identified the components that comprise the relationship of our dreams. Following you'll find the components important to most people:

1. Embody the freedom to be yourself.
2. Offer 100 percent honesty.
3. Do things together.
4. Have fun separately.
5. Allow my mate be free to be him or herself.
6. Try not to control what others say or do.
7. Do not allow others to control me.
8. Enjoy the freedom to have time alone.
9. Be free to spend time with my mate and with friends.
10. Be free to spend time separate from my mate.
11. Work through conflict peacefully.
12. Get on the same page regarding our faith.
13. Have a passionate relationship.
14. Get along with people as best as I can.
15. Be faithful to my mate.

16. Trust my mate is faithful to me.
17. Accept imperfections in my mate without belittling or criticizing.
18. Cultivate feelings of happiness and joyfulness.
19. Be able to express how I feel without criticism or judgment.
20. Accept how my partner feels without criticism or judgment.
21. See my partner and feel seen by my partner.
22. Appreciate that we are friends and like each other.
23. Jealous or demanding behavior is unacceptable.
24. My partner is not jealous or demanding.
25. My partner and I share similar life goals.
26. Laugh together.
27. Feel heard and understood.
28. Work well together.
29. Feel safe with one another physically and emotionally.
30. Respect each other's boundaries.

DEVELOPING AN IDEAL RELATIONSHIP: SESSION 1

We will complete this chapter in one session. Whether you are single, have recently begun a new relationship, or have been in a relationship for a long time, it is beneficial to look at elements that contribute toward an ideal relationship.

When I was young, I intrinsically knew what I wanted in a life partner, but I never knew how to quantify those characteristics. Because of that, key pieces of ideal partner aspects were missing, both in what I brought to the relationship and within my partner. My husband and I are currently having success developing some of those weak areas.

You can avoid some of the pitfalls we encountered and repair the ways your relationship has gone haywire. How?

Consider the qualities you want in your partner. If you are already in a relationship, those weak areas can be developed. If you desire a relationship, have confidence that someone exists with most, if not all, of the qualities you desire. After all, God made an appropriate helper for Adam. He never changes; therefore He will provide the right helper for you too. (Genesis 2:18). Have faith in this truth, and have patience in God as he prepares to bring forth the right relationship in due time. Those qualities can be formed or enhanced by the actions *you choose* to take to develop the characteristics in *yourself* that you seek to find in others. Remember, we are mirrors of one another.[1]

A. Before we dig into this chapter, describe the qualities you desire in a partner by answering the following questions.
1. What type of faith or belief system do you desire in a partner?

2. What physical characteristics most appeal to you?

3. What life goals do you have (dreams, aspirations)?

4. What social status (vocation, educational level) do you desire?

5. What other qualities are important to you?

Rate the percentage the following feel true in your own relationship. (If you are not in a relationship right now, how important are each of the following qualities to you in a future relationship?)

% True	Qualities
_____	Feeling free to be myself
_____	Spending time doing things together
_____	Having fun separately
_____	My partner feels free to be him or herself
_____	No controlling or being controlled
_____	Spending time alone
_____	Spending time with friends, with my mate and separate from my mate
_____	Getting through conflict peacefully
_____	Being on the same page with our faith
_____	Having a passionate relationship
_____	Getting along with most people
_____	Trusting each other
_____	Feeling happy around my partner
_____	Being able to express how I feel without criticism or judgment
_____	Accepting how the other person feels without criticism or judgment
_____	Seeing and be seen by one another
_____	Being close friends and admiring each other's strengths
_____	No jealousy
_____	Having similar life goals
_____	Being able to laugh together
_____	Feeling heard and understood
_____	Working well together
_____	Feeling safe

1. Which of the above qualities did you rate lower than you'd like them to be?

2. What are some things you can do to increase the level of those qualities? By now, you know the answer is not, "Wait for my spouse to change." If you're feeling powerless to make a difference in that area, revisit the chapter on fears. Figure out what you can do to make a difference. What are some options for taking action?

3. What components of an ideal relationship would you add to the above list?

4. Which area is most important for you to focus on improving first?

My prayer over you:

Dear God, I pray for this dear reader as they examine what they can do to work on improving their relationships. Thank You for shifting this reader from powerlessness to empowerment! In Jesus' name, amen.

Conversation starters with God:

Now it's your turn to pray. Find a quiet place. Bring a journal and pen if you enjoy writing your prayers. Above all, be prepared to listen to what God has to say to you in response. And because prayer is a conversation with someone who knows and loves you, here are a few conversations starters to get the ball rolling:

Dear God,
- What do You most want for me to take away from today's session?
- What quality do You want me to work on improving first?
- As a single person, it sometimes seems like all the good ones are taken. Give me a sign that You indeed do have someone for me. What is a sign that will encourage me?
- As a married person with a long history of ditchy behavior in my marriage, it seems like an almost overwhelming task to work on improving the quality of our relationship, especially when I feel like I have to do it all myself. Show me what I need to do that will be effective.

Points to ponder in group discussion or private journaling:
1. As you interacted with God, what did you hear from Him?

2. What was the biggest aha moment from this section?

3. Based on what you learned in this session, identify one action you can take that would be helpful.

AFTERWORD

ROAD TRIP

You are *not* stuck. You really can change how you interact with others, which, in turn, affects how they interact with you. Here are some important reminders:

- You matter! You are free to choose! You are empowered!
- You can become the best version of yourself.
- God is infinitely greater than any fear, and you can overcome all things with His help.
- We are all a work in progress. Forgiveness of both yourself and others is central to healing and healthy relationships.
- Practice do-overs with everyone.
- Trust in God diminishes fear.

ROAD TRIP: SESSION 1

So here you are at the end of this workbook. You are finally ready to head out on your own road trip! The whole point writing *Unstuck* and this accompanying study guide is to get you unstuck. How stuck do you feel now that you've gone through this study guide?

Write that down under "Now" below.

You may have only recently started your journey, or perhaps you feel like you're not completely unstuck yet, but at least you know you're on your way. I've been working on getting unstuck for years. It's a long, slow process, but with every step you will experience more freedom and joy in your life. After you rate how you feel now in the spaces below, return to chapter 1 of the study guide and rewrite your chapter 1 answers below, then calculate the difference:

	NOW	CHAPTER 1 RATING	DIFFERENCE +/-
Rate how stuck you feel:	_____	_____	_____
Rate your level of anxiety:	_____	_____	_____
Rate how fearful you feel:	_____	_____	_____

Even if the rating has improved by only one point, that's significant progress! If it got worse, that means you're far more aware of the fears plaguing you than you were at the start. You also now have tools for addressing those fears. Battle them one at a time. Remember that growing in awareness is change even if behaviors haven't changed yet.

1. What are you aware of now that you were clueless about before you began this study guide?

2. In what ways have you started to change already?

3. What do you notice about your interactions with others? (Remember, sometimes things get worse before they get better. Reflect on this in a positive light.)

4. In what ways has your view of God's ability to help you overcome your fears grown?

5. On what do you need to begin working toward forgiveness of yourself?

6. On what do you need to begin working toward forgiveness of others?

7. In what ways do you need to become more accepting of yourself?

8. In what ways do you need to become more accepting of others?

Consider starting a "Good Things in My life" journal. It takes practice to shift our focus from what's wrong with us, others, and the world to what's true, honest, just, pure, lovely, and of good report (Philippians 4:8).

Have you tried asking for or offering someone a do-over yet?

If not, plan to find an opportunity to try it today.

If you put fear on a continuum on the far left and faith on the far right, mark where would you land on the line right now?

Fear _____ **Faith**

I hope your journey is rich with experiences where you feel more empowered every day, with each day growing more positive. I pray this leads you to embody a peace that passes all understanding on *Your* Road Trip!

My prayer over you:
Dear God, I pray for this dear reader as they work through their difficulties, guiding them to freer, more empowered, happier lives! Please fulfill Your promise to be with each person who completes this study guide. In Jesus' name, amen.

Conversation starters with God:

Now it's your turn to pray. Find a quiet place. Bring a journal and pen if you enjoy writing your prayers. Above all, be prepared to listen to what God has to say to you in response. And because prayer is a conversation with someone who knows and loves you, here are a few conversations starters to get the ball rolling:

Dear God,
- What do You most want for me to take away from today's session?
- What is the overriding point You want me to remember from this study guide?
- Bring to my mind important things I have learned through this process. What are those gems?
- Show me how You have blessed me as I worked through this guide.

Points to ponder in group discussion or private journaling:

1. As you interacted with God, what did you hear from Him?

2. What was the biggest aha moment from this section?

3. Based on what you learned in this session, identify one action you can take that would be helpful.

NOTES

Introduction
1. Ingenuity Films, *Before the Wrath*, accessed March 11, 2022. https://beforethewrath.com.

Chapter 1: The Others-Focused Ditch
1. Get Self Help, https://www.get.gg/docs/TheContainer.pdf.

Chapter 2: The Me-Focused Ditch
1. Schwartz, Richard C. *You Are the One You've Been Waiting For: Bringing Courageous Love to Intimate Relationships* (Center for Self Leadership: 2008), p. 8.

Chapter 6: Deep Ravines
1. California Courts, accessed January 9, 2021, https://www.courts.ca.gov/partners/documents/dvintro1.ppt.

Chapter 9: Stepping-Stones for Crawling Out of the Ditch
1. Robert F. Scuka, William J. Nordling, and Bernard G. Guerney, *Couples' Relationship Enhancement Program Leader's Manual* (Bethesda, MD: IDEALS, Inc., 2004) p. 8.
2. Ibid.
3. Ibid.
4. Flecky, Don and Alexandra (Alex). CoupleTalk. "CoupleTalk: Cracking the Code to an Amazing Relationship!" Last modified March 31, 2019. https://www.coupletalk.com/.

Chapter 10: The ABCDs of Negative Interactions
1. Robert F. Scuka, William J. Nordling, and Bernard G. Guerney, Couples' Relationship Enhancement Program Leader's Manual (Bethesda, MD: IDEALS, Inc., 2004) p.7.

Chapter 11: Path to Empowerment: How to Stop Attacking and Accusing
1. Robert F. Scuka, William J. Nordling, and Bernard G. Guerney, *Couples' Relationship Enhancement Program Leader's Manual* (Bethesda, MD: IDEALS, Inc., 2004) p.7.
2. "Turn Your Words into Gold," Love and Logic Institute, Inc, accessed January 10, 2021, https://www.loveandlogic.com/pages/turn-your-word-into-gold.
3. Robert F. Scuka, William J. Nordling, and Bernard G. Guerney, Couples' Relationship Enhancement Program Leader's Manual (Bethesda, MD: IDEALS, Inc., 2004) p. 17.
4. "Turn Your Words into Gold," Love and Logic Institute, Inc, accessed January 10, 2021, https://www.loveandlogic.com/pages/turn-your-word-into-gold.

Chapter 13: From the Others-Focused Ditch to the Road
1. Robert F. Scuka, William J. Nordling, and Bernard G. Guerney, Couples' Relationship Enhancement Program Leader's Manual (Bethesda, MD: IDEALS, Inc., 2004).

Chapter 14:
1. "Turn Your Words into Gold," Love and Logic Institute, Inc, accessed January 10, 2021, https://www.loveandlogic.com/pages/turn-your-word-into-gold.
2. Ibid.
3. Ibid.

Chapter 16: What to Do About Fear
1. Robert F. Scuka, William J. Nordling, and Bernard G. Guerney, *Couples' Relationship Enhancement Program Leader's Manual* (Bethesda, MD: IDEALS, Inc., 2004).

Chapter 17: Developing an Ideal Relationship

1. Carter-Scott, Cherie. *If Life Is a Game, These Are the Rules: Ten Rules for Being Human as Introduced in Chicken Soup for the Soul.* New York: Harmony, 1999.

ABOUT THE AUTHOR

CHARLENE BENSON is a licensed professional counselor and life coach. She has a private practice in Westminster, Colorado, where she specializes in relationships, trauma, and addictions. She has been using the Ditch People model for more than a decade. This model helps people identify and address extreme behaviors in themselves and others, overcome fears, and find new freedom and happiness in their relationships.

Connect with Charlene at:
www.Facebook.com/CharleneBensonAuthor
cbensonbooks@gmail.com
https://www.cbensonbooks.com

www.ingramcontent.com/pod-product-compliance
Lightning Source LLC
Chambersburg PA
CBHW051802100526
44592CB00016B/2527